Life
After
the Pain:

Breaking the Silence of Abuse

By

Blanca Rosa Romero

Life After the Pain:
Breaking the Silence of Abuse

Copyright © 1999

Scripture quotations are taken from The Student Bible, King James Version, copyright © 1992, 1996 by The Zondervan Corporation

Safe Haven Publishing
P.O. Box 171
Belcamp, Maryland 21017
Ofc: (410) 297-9559
Fax: (410) 297-9560

Cover Design: *Lange Design*
Illustrator: *Luann Bond*
Photo by: *Glamour Shots*
Makeup by: *Mary L. Weeks*
Editor: *Sarah Azizi*

ISBN: 0-9710205-0-7

4th Printing; *Revised Edition*

Printed in the United States by:
Morris Publishing
3212 East Highway 30
Kearney, NE 68847
1-800-650-7888

Dedication

I dedicate this book to the Christ within.

Indeed, *all* things do
work together for good
to them that love God,
to them who are *the called*
according to *his* purpose.
Romans 8:28

To Louise:

*A beautiful and
tender spirit! I am
grateful to have met you!*

Bless you,
Blanca Romero

Blanca Rosa Romero

i

Acknowledgements

To God belongs all praise, honor, and glory for He alone is worthy. The word of God says in Romans 13:7 to give honour to whom honour is due.

I give honorable mention to Lamont, Dee, Jasmine, and Rev. Ann Jefferson. I thank God for our friendship and your support.

I also want to take this opportunity to honor my Editor and friend, Sarah Azizi, for a job well done and for helping to make this project the best it could possibly be.

Thank you to all the following churches for allowing me the honor to minister the word of God: Colonial Baptist Church, Eastern United Methodist Church, Zion Baptist Church of Christ, True Love Ministries, Brokenness to Wholeness Ministries, and Faith United Baptist Church. Special *thank you* to WLIF, Heaven 600, WRBS, WJRO, WBGR, and WOLB for the live interviews on your stations.

Last, but certainly not least, I give honorable mention to the following organizations for their support and encouragement: Governor's Office of Crime Control & Prevention, Charles H. Hickey, Jr. School, U.S. States Attorney's Office, University of Maryland Public Safety, Frederick Douglass High School, Maryland Network Against Domestic Violence, Family Crisis Center, Maryland Coalition Against Sexual Assault, Men Against Domestic Violence, Family & Children Services of Central Maryland, Maryland Department of Juvenile Justice, Hope Abounds, National Organization for Victim Assistance (NOVA), Baltimore County Department of Social Services, and Domestic Violence Center of Howard County.

Remember, "It's not about me, it's time for **Jesus Christ** to be glorified!!!"

I *love* you all. May God richly bless you.

Let Us Pray

Father Mother God, Thank You! In the precious name and consciousness of Jesus the Christ, we turn within recognizing the **only** power in the universe, God the good, omnipotent, the everywhere – present spirit of absolute good.

Gracious Father, with humility of heart too great to express in words, we use our tongue to say, "Thank You." Father, forgive us. Forgive our erroneous thinking. Forgive our judgments and criticisms against others and ourselves. We honor your tender mercy, loving kindness, and favor.

For a world pre-arranged to provide us our every need, "Thank You." We recognize you provision for every stage of our growth: food, clothing, and shelter. For tools of wisdom in the forms of parents and relatives, siblings and peers, neighbors and teachers, for counselors, friends, colleagues, and clergy, "Thank You."

Daddy, we pray in the wonderful awareness of Jesus the Christ that you will richly bless our President and government officials all over the world; in the United States and other countries alike, pastors, lay ministry leaders, parents, grandparents, extended family members, children of all ages, homeless and hungry, and all of your earthly creations alike.

We thank you that we are free to study, free to worship, free to learn, free to give, free from want and limitation. We are free to see through spiritual eyes, hear through spiritual ears, live according to spiritual law. We are free to image our good, project our good, and accept our good. We do not take any of these freedoms lightly. We appreciate each one as a *gift* from you. We know that these are the birthrights of everyone in the world, and no law or statute can keep this from being so. So, today we celebrate our freedom.

Jesus, our Savior and the Master Teacher, we believe that you are sending forth answers to this prayer as we stand in agreement with all those who will read this book. In the *powerful* nature and consciousness of Jesus' we pray, and so it is, Amen and Amen.

CONTENTS

I Used To Be A Victim

The nights seemed endless,
every touch chipping away,
dreams, visions, and goals,
leaving behind pain, guilt, shame, and fear.
Distorting my mind,
violating my body,
crippling my spirit.
Nobody noticed, nobody cared,
at least, that's how it felt.
A shattered past,
filled with broken promises,
"Now What?" I ask.
Pick up the pieces,
Get around it,
work past it,
and go through it.
But, it takes time,
"What am I left to do in the meantime?"
Well, make the choice that's right for me,
hold onto *his* unchanging hand,
detach myself from the result,
and remember that I was created with a purpose in mind.
He's the same yesterday, today, and forevermore,
He's always available,
never an answering service,
no busy signals,
and, always waiting for my call.
I placed the call,
and today I can proudly say,
I used to be a victim,
now, I am a survivor!

God Bless!

Prologue

Matthew 6:33
But seek ye first the kingdom of God, and his righteousness;
and all these things shall be added unto you.

Have you ever wondered what life would be like after the pain? For many years my favorite saying has been that I'm waiting for life after the pain; in fact, that is how I developed the title for this book through the indwelling presence of God within. It was His great big idea.

Pain is not always physical. Physical pain is indeed terrible, but my personal belief is that the emotional and mental pain associated with sexual and physical abuse is far more traumatic and tends to have a lasting, more horrific effect on your mind.

I've heard people say that physical and sexual abuse keeps you in emotional bondage your entire life. As you journey with me through the account of my life, you will see what effects the abuse I sustained caused in my life. Most importantly, what I want to convey to you is that no matter what I may have suffered at the hands of an abusive stepfather, when I turned within to recognize the presence of God within, all that pain I lived with for years had no choice but to flee. The light had been turned on inside.

I greet you in the name and consciousness of Jesus the Christ; I am Blanca Rosa Romero, and the Author of this book.

I survived many different levels of abuse from the age of two to thirty. The abuse ranged from parental neglect and abandonment to physical and sexual abuse. If you have endured any form of abuse, be it the same or some other form, I want to encourage you to survive; I want you to know that there is *life after the pain.*

This book has been written to share my testimony of how God can take a sorrow and turn it into something beautiful. For by the word of my testimony, your life shall be *prayerfully* transformed.

We are His workmanship,
created in Christ Jesus for good works,
which God prepared beforehand
that we should walk in them.

(Ephesians 2:10)

Please note a few things about this scripture. First, it states that you are God's workmanship. The word in original Greek, in which the verse was written, literally means "a person of notable excellence." He

2

calls you a person of notable excellence because *He made you*. We need to see ourselves as God sees us – a prized example of His creation.

There is one important key to survival, and that is to turn within to recognize and obey the indwelling presence of God. He is the divine answer to any challenge you could ever face. I recognized God as the head of my life on October 23, 1983, and the entire situation of constant rape and physical abuse came to a halt. Earlier that year, I sustained the last account of physical and sexual abuse that I would be subjected to at the hands of my stepfather.

I've survived too many terrible events to count and I'm encouraging you that you too can survive with the grace of our Lord Jesus Christ (2 Cor. 12:9). Many times along the journey of pain, I wanted to give up on life and commit suicide. Several times I tried to end my life, but was unsuccessful. I realized that it wasn't my decision to make; I'm here for the mere existence of God and he shall indeed direct my paths if I trust in Him.

Trust in the Lord with all thine heart;
and lean not unto thine own understanding.
In all thy ways acknowledge Him,
and He shall direct thy paths.
(Proverbs 3:5-6)

Today, I try my best to live my life according to his purpose. I have fulfilled my purpose by turning the light on in a dark situation and breaking the silence it held over my life for many years. I believe that all things do indeed work together for good to those that love God (Romans 8:28).

Abuse is abuse, remember that! Even if you only suffered one aspect of abuse as opposed to multiple forms, please read on because I believe that no matter what sort of violation you sustained, it was wrong and you didn't deserve it!

I assure you that through careful study of the bible, I've arrived at several conclusions. First of all, it was never God's desire that His children be abused psychologically, verbally, spiritually, physically, or sexually. Intense verbal criticism, beatings, and severe deprivation of basic needs (food, shelter, clothing) are emotional and/or physical abuse.

I lived with years of guilt and shame over the abuse, blaming myself and making excuses. I used to think if I had only done something differently, as I'm sure many have thought, things would have been different. The only thing that could have made it turn out differently would be to have chosen a different route to travel.

It's not your fault that you were abused; your heavenly father doesn't blame you nor should you blame yourself. Rest assured that God will deal with those who are abusers in His own time.

To me belongeth vengeance, and recompence;
their foot shall slide in due time;
for the day of their calamity is at hand,
and the things that shall come upon them make haste.
(Deuteronomy 32:35)

You are a child of God and He loves you. I used to believe that if God loved me, then he wouldn't have allowed me to suffer as I was. I know that many survivors have asked themselves, *if God loved me, why would he have allowed me to suffer?* The answer to that question is that God never created you to be abused in any shape, form, or fashion.

One day I was prompted by the Holy Spirit to call on the Lord to save me from a horrific trail of physical beatings with a baseball bat. My stepfather had beat me with a homemade baseball bat for six days; but on the *seventh* day, I was provided a way of escape by the Lord (1 Corinthians 10:13) just as God's word instructs. One thing is for sure: I cried out for God to save me and He did exactly that! I want you to know that He does hear the cries of His children and He will send deliverance just when you desire it most.

I believe that God may not always come when you want Him to, but He will always be right on time. Indeed, He was right on time on March 29, 1983.

And the Lord shall deliver me from every evil work,
and will preserve me unto his heavenly kingdom;
to whom be glory forever and ever.

4

Prologue

(2 Timothy 4:18)

You are not alone. You are not the first woman to experience abuse. And you are not crazy. You didn't ask for it and you didn't do anything to deserve it.

Please, I invite you feed upon the strength I've gained through my own personal experiences. I've learned that what I was searching for could not be found in external objects (sex, drinking, eating, or shopping). It was within me the whole time, but I had to surrender my will to His will in order for the peace of God to take over.

Your strength, as my strength, will only come from the everlasting arms of God. *God is my strength and power; and he maketh my way perfect* (2 Samuel 22:33).

All abuse survivors need hope and healing; emotionally, psychologically, relationally, and physically. To some degree most of us need healing from negative family messages about our lives, regardless whether the offense was big or small, intentional or unintentional, only once or repeatedly.

You may have developed ways to cope with the violence in your life. Many women minimize the abuse in their past as a way of coping with the pain they are left to resolve on their own. The dynamics of power and control are at work in many abusive situations and may make it difficult to tell someone. You, like many other women, may want the abuse to end but don't know where to turn, or feel too embarrassed to admit the problem to anyone. Maybe you can't even admit it to yourself.

Few if any of us were blessed with the perfect family: a loving father, nurturing mother, supportive siblings, and admiring relatives. But the word of God says that when your mother and father forsake you, he will take you up (Psalm 27:10). All you must do is turn within.

I urge you to take heart in the matter. The word of the Lord tells us that by his stripes we are healed (1 Peter 2:24). Therefore, there's redemption and freedom in God's *healing* hands.

In this book, you will travel with me through my young adult life, to when I was married to my first husband, and read how the marriage ended in divorce, as well as many other storms of my life.

5

I'll discuss issues of importance for abuse survivors such as telling the truth versus lying, trust, faith, deliverance, friendships, and forgiveness. The Lord inspired me to write on these topics because he wants us to be completely free in our walk with him. For when Jesus sets you free, you are free indeed (John 8:36).

I'll tell you where I am today and how I'm still learning that "*Yes, there is life after the pain!*" Remember, it takes daily effort on your part to endure the challenges of this lifetime. Please, remember to be *patient* with yourself in your attempt to recover from the pain of your past. I want you to keep one thing in your mind, if you have ever been a victim: you are not a victim anymore; see yourself as a survivor! One basic message is that man, through his God nature, can be a victor of circumstance, rather than a victim. That no matter what may happen, man can learn to cope with and overcome any and all challenges of life.

Do not allow your past to dictate your future! But remember, it will take much prayer and much fasting. A former co-worker of mine shared with me a poem full of truth:

> *"Much Prayer equals Much Power*
> *Little Prayer equals Little Power*
> *No Prayer equals No Power"*

Please journey with me into my life, with compassion and an open mind.

God richly bless!

Chapter 1

I Wasn't Born A Boy

Psalm 139:13-14
*For thou hast possessed my reins:
thou hast covered me in my mother's womb. I will praise thee;
for I am fearfully and wonderfully made:
marvellous are thy works;
and that my soul knoweth right well.*

Life After the Pain

July 24, 1967 at 9:01 a.m.: another little girl arrived upon the earth. I was unplanned, unexpected, and unwanted by both of my parents.

Normally, parents are happy to have a newborn baby in their lives. My father, however, left my mother immediately upon my arrival. I was told that if he had to have a child, he wanted it to be a son. My parents were married at the time but a child was definitely not part of the bargain. These were the circumstances of my entrance into this world.

In the inconvenience of being left husbandless and with a child, my mother became very angry with me. She decided to drop me off at my Grandmother's house, but Grandma was not interested in raising a baby either. I can only imagine how I felt, being shifted from home to home, not feeling loved or wanted by anyone. It's assumed that babies are unaware of what is going on in their surroundings, but I disagree. I believe that the surrounding in a baby's life becomes a part of her. One may not be able to see it by just looking at the person, but those memories do surface.

Grandma turned me over to my aunt, who agreed to care for me. I don't really remember a lot about living with my aunt, but I assume it was pleasant.

My mother returned two years later, and wanted to assume the responsibility of her child with a newfound love; my aunt had no alternative but to hand me over to my mother as she didn't have legal custody.

My mother took me to our new home in Baltimore and told me that the man living there was my father. I didn't know any better and accepted the possibility that he could be my father. To a two-year-old, it doesn't matter who someone is; it only matters that he, or she, loves you.

All of a sudden, I went from having two parents who cared nothing for me to having two parents who were going to attempt to provide a good home for me. All I wanted was to be with my family and have someone show me love.

I was a dysfunctional child, two years old and not yet potty-trained. Many things were missing from my life and the results showed up in many forms. I guess the abandonment issues were surfacing through my inability, or lack of willingness, to use the potty.

My stepfather and mother were very frustrated by my disobedience to use the potty and soon thereafer the physical abuse began. They would beat me in hopes of forcing me to use the potty, but it only caused me to become rebellious. I had never been beaten prior to this so, as a two-year-old child, I didn't have a clue as to why they wanted to hurt me.

Abusive mothers, fathers, or relatives teach children that their bodies are worthless for anything except a beating. If a mother can beat and bruise her child so readily; if a father can sexually violate the child so easily; if the child feels as though she doesn't matter to her parents; then the child begins to think she doesn't matter to anyone. Usually the child will believe that if she behaved differently, the abuse wouldn't occur, and its aftershocks torment the child, even into adulthood.

I believe that I was subconsciously angry with them for leaving me and I figured the best way to get them back was not to use the potty. It only angered them and they would beat me with belts, vacuum cleaner cords, tree branches, or whatever they could get their hands on. Yes, in the beginning, beatings were a joint effort between my parents.

I have memories of going to kindergarten with bruises covering my legs from top to bottom, including my behind. It was difficult to sit down with those bruises on my body and I was yelled at by the teacher to take a seat or go to the principal's office. Well, I was rebellious so I refused to sit down because it hurt too badly.

The teachers didn't know I was being abused and I was too embarrassed to say anything in front of the other students. I was embarrassed that I couldn't sit down because my legs were covered with welts from the vacuum cleaner cords and tree branches. I later tried to tell my teachers, one on one, but nobody would listen.

Needless to say, I ended up in the principal's office. I was disciplined verbally to obey my teacher. I tried to tell the principal why I was unable to sit down but he wasn't willing to listen either. To the school officials, I was just a problem child. I felt like nobody believed me about the beatings nor did anyone care to investigate or even look at my bruises. As you see, the events that occurred thus far were beginning to effect my thinking patterns.

I remember being teased by my classmates for being sent to the principal's office so frequently. My classmates used to scream out that I was a bad child; they didn't have a clue that I was being beaten by my stepfather. I never felt comfortable telling them because I was embarrassed. I didn't want to be rejected; I wanted to be accepted.

Some days when I'd go to school, I didn't know what I'd have to face that day. There were days that I'd get beat up by my classmates because I looked different. Can you imagine how I felt coming from a home where I was abused and walking into a school being abused?

I went to the nurse's office at least once a week to complain about the beatings and the nurse would just send me back to my classroom. I'd go to the nurse and complain about being beat up by the kids and nothing was ever done about it. All I ever did was end up back in the classroom; I was teased and beat up again.

In my young mind, I was not a problem child because, despite the abuse at home and the lack of concern for my well-being by school officials, I was an honor-roll student enrolled in the "Gifted and Talented Program." You see, I had potential, had I only been given the proper direction in life. I maintained that educational status throughout elementary school, in spite of the innumerable incidents of abuse by my parents and classmates.

I can remember running away once to a classmate's home after school. I was covered, as usual, with bruises all over my buttocks and legs. I was embarrassed but I remember thinking that perhaps someone might finally listen to me and help. My body was covered with black and blue welp bruises from a beating with the vacuum cleaner cord. My classmate's mother called the police and reported what I told her and the police came to pick me up. Unfortunately, they brought me back home to my parents. The police told my parents that I was making up stories of abuse and trying to make trouble for my family. They didn't even check to see if I had any bruises on my body at the time. We call that "inadequate job performance" today.

Once again, my cries for help were ignored by the police, who were sworn to protect the innocent! Remember: this still happens today!

I believe that time after time, the Lord was giving me a way of escape, but the people who should have been protecting me were not willing. Instead, they sent me back to the cruel hands of my parents.

The abuse from my parents, particularly my stepfather, increased to a phenomenal level. The beatings became regular and consistent. Each day when he arrived home from work, he'd find a reason to beat me and if he wasn't beating me, he was beating my mother.

Many times as a child, I witnessed my mother being abused by my stepfather. I witnessed my mother tumbling down the stairs from being pushed by my stepfather. I wish you could imagine how that felt, to see my mother getting the crap beat out of her and feeling helpless because there was nothing I could do to protect her. I felt guilty for many years about the abuse she sustained from this man. However, I kept thinking: she's an adult, she should be able to make a decision that could protect both of us – but she didn't. She was too afraid of him; it took me a long time to figure that out.

Our house was filled with rage, the anger of a man who claimed to love us. The only way he knew how to display his love was through his fist or by slapping us around. He abused both of us, one no worse than the other in my eyes.

I feel that abuse is abuse; my mother and I didn't deserve any of the abuse that we sustained at the hands of this monster who claimed to love us. I felt completely helpless in the matter because I couldn't protect my mother or myself.

My mother seemed petrified of him. He had gained control of her mind. She seemed so scared of him that she couldn't muster up the courage to remove us from that hostile environment. I remember asking her to take us somewhere away from him and her response was "he loves us." I couldn't relate to that kind of love and I still don't agree with that. I believe I knew back then that I was a child of God and didn't deserve

11

that kind of treatment from anyone. I definitely know today that abuse doesn't add up to love.

I kept hoping, however, that one day my mother would get enough back bone to pick me up and save our lives. All she did was make excuse after excuse for his behavior. She protected this man, and I kept wondering, even as a child, "Why do we stay here?"

Each time I left and was sent back, the abuse intensified tenfold. I never felt like it was home; I never felt as though I belonged there. I asked my mother on numerous occasions if I could go back and live with my aunt and she would say no. Then she would start guilting me about how ungrateful I was acting. She would say: *he bought us a home and you should be thankful.* How do you bring yourself to tell a five-year-old child to be grateful for getting beatings everyday? Still, I think, could someone please explain that to me?

When my stepfather was away from home, my mother would just sit in her room and cry. She obviously was miserable living this way and I never understood why she wouldn't just leave. He'd beat her so viciously, like she was a dog. In fact, I've never seen anyone beat their dog the way he beat my mother and me.

I was beat almost every morning before I left for school and again when I returned home. I began to believe that he must love me or he wouldn't spend so much time beating me. The whole clincher of it, for me, was that he wasn't a drinker or drug-user, so addiction was never an excuse.

I spent most of my alone time crying, afraid of what might happen next. My stepfather kept a gun in the house, and my worst fear was that one day I'd come home from school and find my mother lying in a pool of blood. I also feared that maybe she'd come home and find me in a pool of blood. I don't know which one I feared more.

I remember getting in the way a couple of times when he was beating her and he threw me across the room and told me to mind my own business. My mother was my business. Despite her lack of protection for me, I still tried to protect her – I always ended up with more bruises.

In fact, one time he was threatening my mother with his gun, and I was afraid that my worst nightmare was about to come true, so I jumped in front of my mother to save her. I remember thinking if he had to kill someone, let it be me. It angered him and he punched me on my forehead with his fist. My forehead starting bleeding profusely and I thought I was going to die because he had a ring on with a large stone and it created a big gash on my forehead.

They never took me to the hospital to have my forehead stitched, but it did eventually heal. I didn't run away that time because I was too afraid that if he found me, he'd kill me. I guess deep down inside, I didn't want to die.

Not only was I being physically abused at this time and not offered protection by anyone, I was also verbally abused in school by my classmates. I was verbally assaulted by my classmates because I was the product of a mixed couple and that was not accepted in the seventies. I'd go home, tell my parents, and was offered no compassion by them; in fact, I can remember them laughing at me. My stepfather only offered physical violence as a solution. Once, he told me to go to school and fight the kids that called me names.

The next day I got into a fight with one of my classmates over the dirty names she called me. I had so much pent up anger over the abuse I was suffering at home that I lost my mind when I was fighting that girl. I tried to beat her like my stepfather was beating me.

I felt guilty for beating up that girl, but on the other hand, I was tired of being abused by everyone. I did what I felt I had to do at the time. I'm not proud of how I acted. I wish I knew then what I know now, that two wrongs never make a right.

My parents always stuck me in the middle of their arguments, whenever they didn't agree with one another. It was clear that my parents had not grown up, by the way they acted and the way they treated me. When I didn't have an opinion, I sustained incredible beatings. I constantly felt like I was in a tug-of-war game between the two of them. My stepfather always tried to coherce me into protecting him instead of my mother and my mother did the same. I couldn't win on either side; either way I was doomed, destined for a beating.

I remember when I was *seven* years old, I had a little German shepherd puppy. I can still see his cute little face. I loved that puppy because my stepfather bought it for me for my birthday. One day, the puppy fell down the stairs in the basement and even though I tried, I couldn't save it. I was beat so terribly that night, because my stepfather thought I intentionally killed my puppy. Can you imagine being a seven-year-old child accused of murder?

To know me is to know that I'd never harm a fly, at least not intentionally. I was brutally beaten on my arms, legs, and buttocks because my stepfather believed I deliberately killed the puppy.

Soon after I turned eight years old, we moved from Baltimore to a beautiful home in Harford County. I used to dream that the abuse would stop now that we were not in the same environment anymore. Perhaps brighter days lay ahead in this beautiful home situated in a nice quiet neighborhood of Joppatowne, Maryland.

I was looking forward to new beginnings and leaving the past behind. At least, I was hopeful that that was what lay ahead for my mother and me.

Chapter 2

A Move I'll Never Forget

---

2 Corinthians 1:4
Who comforteth us in all our tribulation,
that we may be able to comfort them which are in any trouble,
by the comfort wherewith we ourselves are comforted of God.

Wrong answer! The beatings were packed up in one of the boxes and one night soon after we moved in, they found their way out of the box. Indeed, I was wrong because I thought once the environment changed that the abuse would stop, but that was just another in a long line of failed hopes.

One night, my stepfather started beating me with tree branches again. My legs seemed to be in more pain than they ever had been. I always thought maybe it was the tree branches in the county versus the branches in the city. Pretty silly, huh? I realize now that sometimes you have to think silly thoughts in order to keep yourself from going insane.

Anyhow, my beatings were picking up where they left off, and for no particular reason other than he had had a bad day. I received a beating at least every other day, some days worse than others. Some days the beatings would last five minutes; others, an hour or more. My legs felt like someone lit a torch and was literally burning my flesh. As I hear the account of Jesus' death, I feel I can understand what it felt like as they beat him 39 times, ripping his flesh off his bones. That is exactly what my stepfather was doing to me.

After reading the account of Jesus' death told in Matthew 27, I realize that nothing I endured compares to the torture and humiliation rendered upon our Lord and Savior, Jesus Christ.

I was nearing nine years old when my mother had a baby, a beautiful little girl. She was the most beautiful creation I'd seen. Each time I looked at her I wondered in the back of my mind, "Will she be subjected to harm by my stepfather someday?" I remember being so afraid, wondering, *will he beat her the way he beats me?*

Nevertheless, she brought a lot of joy into my life by her mere existence. Her arrival had taken, at least for a few months, some focus, away from the beatings I was receiving every other day. Since the arrival of my baby sister, my stepfather only beat me about once a week; he seemed happy to have a new face in the house. He spent a lot of time with my sister. I understood completely because she was a gem from heaven above!

Fourteen months after my sister's arrival, I had a little brother. I was just getting used to having her around and now I had two babies in the house! It didn't matter, though, because I was overjoyed by their presence.

Once again, I was getting beatings every day of the week. Sometimes the bruises from the previous beating hadn't even healed when new bruises were pounded onto my body. My flesh was bleeding daily and just as scabs began to form, new beatings ripped the newly formed scabs right off my skin.

I ran away. I went over to a classmate's home and spent the night there without the knowledge of her parents. The next day, my friend convinced me to go and report the abuse to the police. I didn't want to because I knew they wouldn't protect me, but I went anyway and filed a report with the local police department in Harford County. To my surprise, they listened to my complaints, telephoned the local Department of Social Services (DSS) and had me picked up.

DSS removed me from the home and placed me in foster care pending a thirty day investigation. Thirty days later, I was returned to the abusive home based on the fact that DSS couldn't secure sufficient evidence to keep me from the home any longer. I must inform you that when I initially went to the police department and was referred to DSS, my legs and buttocks were covered with black/blue bruises, so they had sufficient evidence from my point of view. As I was en route back home again, I remember thinking to myself, "Nobody believes me because they're sending me back to the enemy yet again." My life seemed hopeless, as though I was destined for beatings the rest of my life. What kind of way is that for a ten-year-old to think? I had no other alternative.

Arrival back at home thirty days later was terrible! My stepfather was angry with me for running away and reporting the abuse to the authorities. I was petrified because I knew that the beatings were going to continue. I always thought that by the authorities sending me back, it symbolized to his sick mind that it was okay for him to abuse me.

He told me that he missed me and thought he had lost me for good. The beatings actually stopped for about a month, and my legs and buttocks had some much needed time for healing.

My mother was a very cold woman, never showed any love toward me. My stepfather only knew how to show love through tree branches, belts, or vacuum cleaner cords meshed against my flesh, literally ripping it apart. It still hurts to think about how unavailable they were for me as a child, but I recognize now that all I can do is pray for them.

My sister and brother were still babies and I enjoyed the precious moments that we were permitted to share with one another. When I came back home from running away, my stepfather would not allow me to spend an excessive amount of time with the babies, saying that I might influence them to become problem children like I was.

My worst fear became reality one day when he began to physically abuse my sister and brother. I witnessed their beatings with the extension cords and I tried desperately to defend them, which was more than I could say for our mother. I can't even find the words to express to you how it felt to see him beat those babies like he did. It was horrific! They would cry and scream out for our mother; she would just stand by and cry. I can still hear their cries today as I write this account. My mother protected no one from the abuse.

In their defense, I received many beatings, and I didn't mind, as long as it wasn't them. Once again, his anger ruled him and he'd beat me worse than he probably would have beaten them. My body had built up resistance to the pain after so many years of abuse. Don't get me wrong, I still felt the pain, but I'd simply imagine I was somewhere else and tune out mentally from the beating. Later in therapy, I was told that that is a normal reaction for victims of abuse.

Life returned to its normal status before the arrival of my siblings. I was back to being beaten at least every other day. Nothing changed but the pictures on the calendar.

Chapter 3

Nightmare in Baltimore

Matthew 19:29
*And every one that hath forsaken houses,
or brethren, or sisters, or father, or mother, or wife, or children,
or lands, for my name's sake,
shall receive an hundredfold, and shall inherit everlasting life.*

Life After the Pain

woke up because we had been in a terrible car accident. I must
have been about ten and a half years old at the time.

My entire family was in the car. We were on our way back to
Baltimore from Virginia, where we had been visiting our extended family.
My sister, brother and I were okay, just a little shaken up.

My mother was severely injured; her leg was partially severed in
the accident. We spent that night in the hospital and I remember my
stepfather sitting by my side telling me that everything was going to be
fine. He expressed how much he loved me and how he was worried
about me.

It puzzled me, why he was sitting with me rather than with my
mother. I kept thinking that maybe my mother had passed away and they
just didn't want to tell me. It turned out that my mother was alive but
was having emergency surgery performed on her legs.

A couple of days later we returned home from the hospital. My
mother had a cast on her leg from her hip down to her ankle. She
couldn't walk up the stairs at all so my stepfather set up the family room
so she could sleep downstairs. He didn't sleep with her, though, he kept
sleeping upstairs.

Little to my knowledge, my stepfather had a new agenda.

After the accident, I was beaten less often, and I began to think
he had changed. If I had had a choice, I would have taken daily beatings
rather than his new form of abuse.

One night while I was in the upstairs bathroom, he came in and
asked me to sit on his lap, claiming he needed to talk with me. When I
sat down he started to forcefully kiss me in my mouth. I started crying
and questioned, what was he doing to me, and why? He told me he was
lonely and needed affection. He said he loved me and was sorry for all
the beatings. I was completely confused. Deep down inside, something
told me that what he was doing was wrong.

My stepfather used to tell me how beautiful he thought I was.
He made frequent comments about the growth of my body parts but I'd
just ignore the comments and leave the room.

20

I didn't pay attention to his comments until after the first incident occurred in the bathroom. My relationship with my own body was now filled with tension and unease because of his sexual advances toward me. I began thinking that my looks had brought on the abuse. I developed feelings of shame for being attractive. I desperately wished that I wasn't attractive and I started a course of overeating to gain weight. I remember thinking that if I were overweight, perhaps he'd lose interest.

A few days later, I was in my bedroom when he came in and asked me to sit on his lap again. I had a quick flashback to the other night and immediately told him that I would not comply with his request. He told me he was going to beat me if I didn't listen to what he told me to do. At this point I didn't care if he beat me or not because I had become numb from all the abuse. Well, he left my room.

I heard him go into the bathroom and run some bath water. I didn't think about it again until he returned to my room and asked me to come to the bathroom with him. I now complied with this request in pure fear. When I walked into the bathroom I could see that the water in the tub was very, very hot because of the steam rising from it. He demanded that I get into the tub but I refused. The only option I was offered by him was to surrender my body and will to him.

After my refusal, he immediately picked me up and forced me into the bathtub with my pajamas on causing my head to go under the water. By the force of his hand upon my chest, it felt as though I was going to drown. He finally decided to let me up and pulled me out of the tub and threw me onto the floor. As I was lying there I felt as though my entire body was on fire.

He didn't offer me any comfort nor did he show any compassion for what he had just done to me. Did I actually expect him to? I had no idea that he wasn't finished yet. The next thing I remember was him not only exposing but releasing himself on me. At that moment I was stripped of my self-esteem, pride, dignity, respect, peace, and joy.

It was a horrible experience to endure. First he was trying to kill me and then, maybe for a moment, he changed his mind and decided to allow me to live. I now believe it was the Lord who stopped him from drowning me in the bathtub. He didn't violate my insides that night but he tortured me with his indignities.

Later that night I ran away and, instead of going to the police, I decided to walk the streets. I passed by the woods on Joppa Farm Road, not far from my parent's home, and decided to sleep there. It was very cold outside so I nestled in some leaves and cried myself to sleep.

I woke up the next morning and decided to go report the incident in the bathroom to the police. The only thing the police did was call my stepfather and ask him to come and pick me up from the police station. I felt so alone and I knew the law didn't have any interest in protecting me from this man. Once again, the child was thrown back into the hands of the enemy. How many times would the authorities return me back to this home? Were they setting me up for my death? These are the questions I lived with throughout my adolescent years. For I know that the enemy comes only to steal, and to kill, and to destroy (John 10:10).

Upon returning home, he dragged me out to the woods behind our house and proceeded to look for a branch that he could beat me with; he insisted that I help him find one. I received my good old beating like I had in the past, and was left with numerous bruises and welts, and my legs were bleeding.

He was angry with me for running away. Why wouldn't I have run away? Anybody with any courage would have done the same.

My mother was still wearing her cast, which she wore for almost a year. When she heard of my accusation she only hurled insults at me, saying that I was just a "trouble maker, whore and a slut, looking for attention." Imagine for a moment how you would feel if your mother was making those accusations after you've been brutally beaten by your stepfather. Please forgive me if those names are offensive to you, but I heard them for years, growing up in that home.

I thought: what a way for a mother to talk to her own daughter? Her first born child for whom she had no regard whatsoever. But in the back of my mind I knew that I didn't matter anymore now than what I meant before my sister and brother were born. She didn't protect me then and she wasn't going to protect me now. I had to grow up and start defending myself the best way I knew how.

Mother's cast was removed and she was able to eventually gain enough strength to walk upstairs. She did so at her earliest opportunity. She began to spend less and less time with me, eventually ignoring me completely. If I tried to solicit her attention, she'd just yell that she wanted nothing to do with me and followed that comment by slamming the door in my face.

Throughout my childhood, I can clearly remember the sound of doors being slammed in my face by my parents when they didn't want to be bothered with me.

One night, while in my bedroom sleeping and probably dreaming about something pleasant, I was awakened by my stepfather on top of me, trying to force himself in my mouth. I started screaming and yelling for him to get off of me. My mother came to my bedroom door and asked him to stop whatever he was trying to do and to come back to bed. He got up and as he was leaving my room he said, "Don't worry, I'll be back later."

I heard him go into my mother's room with her and they started arguing. For the first time in my eleven years of life, my mother finally showed some compassion and tried to protect me. I remember thinking maybe she had a change of heart. Would she actually begin to protect her child? Hmm....

As promised, he returned to my room a couple of hours later and woke me up, forcing his manhood into my untouched innocence. I immediately screamed, hoping my mother would come to my rescue again. She never did. I guess she changed her mind about protecting me. He was successful in his robbery of all that I had. The next thought I remember was, "I'm going to kill this man or send him to jail, one or the other." He raped me and there's not a pretty way to say that. I know people don't enjoy hearing gruesome details about rape, but there is nothing pleasant about being brutally raped.

He now had taken this abuse to a whole new level. After he committed the ultimate sin of incest and adultery against my mother, he

23

left my room and left me there crying and bleeding. There was no sign of compassion or regret for what he had done. Then again, why would he start to care at that point?

The next day I tried to talk to my mother about what happened and she told me that she didn't want to know about it, and didn't care. *How could she be so insensitive? Why didn't she protect me?*

I told her that he had taken complete advantage of me when he came back to my bedroom the second time. She then got a bar of soap and forced me to eat it, and told me I needed to wash my mouth out of all those lies I just told her. That soap was nasty and every time I tried to tell her something he tried to do, she'd make me eat another bar of Ivory soap. Needless to say, after about three bars of soap I stopped telling her. I began to think that maybe it wasn't wrong because she didn't seem to care one way or another. I was confused because I was still just a child.

He continued to come into my room in the middle of the night and force himself upon me. He violated every area of my body that he could. All the innocence of an eleven-year-old child had been stripped away from me in a matter of minutes. There wasn't any part of my body that he didn't violate. I would scream out for help but nobody came to my rescue. Whatever this man wanted to do to me, it didn't matter because nobody was going to stop him. After he would leave my bedroom, I would lay there the rest of the night bleeding and trembling in pure fear.

I decided to run away again after his violations, and inform the police. The police listened and called DSS to come and pick me up. The Harford County Department of Social Services removed me from the home for a thirty-day investigation. It was determined at the hospital that my innocence had indeed been stripped away and parts of him were detected on the inside. The bruises that laced my legs and buttocks were photographed and placed in the police records. I was placed with a different foster home this time. Initially, the family was very nice and loving towards me. I remember the mother bought me an all white bunny rabbit. I named her "Fluffy." She was beautiful and loved to play.

But, trauma seemed to follow me wherever I went. Their son tried to rape me. He wasn't successful because I started screaming and he called me a "chicken." I remember him saying to me that, "All the girls that come to live there surrender themselves to me; especially the rape victims!" I told his mother what he did and said to me, and I was subsequently removed from that home. In case you're wondering, nothing was ever done to the son for the attempted rape. I was simply removed and placed in yet another foster home, totaling three at this point.

Now I didn't feel I belonged anywhere; I didn't have any place to call "home." I was notified after moving to the third home that they were planning to send me back to my family. Social Services said that they were unable to come up with sufficient evidence against my stepfather to hold up in a court of law. I also overheard the social worker saying to the foster mother: "She's a problem child and we'll have difficulty placing her anywhere." The social worker was referring to me. Now, what kind of statement is that to hear from someone who should be on your side?

The authorities would often accuse me of "not having my story straight." They were referring to the times that I ran away and would tell them about the abuse that occurred. According to the authorities, I always told a different story. I did tell different stories, because each time the abuse I had sustained was, in fact, different from the last time in many ways.

I couldn't believe this, *how much more evidence did they need?* This had to be the most unreal story I'd ever heard from authorities. In fact, it had to be a dream! The authorities had photographs of my bruises, a proven test that my hymen had ruptured, and a test that proved that there were manly secretions inside of me. Yet, they said there wasn't sufficient evidence.

Back home again, I was returned to the foul nature of that household. This time my mother was very angry with me and enticed my stepfather to beat me in order to make me stop running away. He didn't have a problem complying with that request. Actually he seemed to enjoy beating me that day, laughing with every strike against my flesh.

25

He beat me with a vacuum cleaner cord and this beating was very intense; each lash felt like it penetrated my soul. My mother definitely didn't have the best interests of her child in mind. She disliked me with every part of her being.

Her encouragement to beat me escalated the abuse to hitherto untouched heights because it symbolized to him that he had nothing to worry about. He instilled so much fear in my mother that she would never defy him; she would always protect him.

I ran away again that night. I told the police that I'd been brutally beaten again and asked for their assistance. My arms, legs, back, and buttocks were laced with lacerations from the vacuum cleaner cord. Some were bleeding because my skin was actually ripped! I was photographed, and again removed from the home. Needless to say, thirty days later I was returned home. When would someone listen and stop risking my life? Over and over again, all DSS did was remove me for thirty days and send me back again.

My stepfather continued to brutally rape and beat me. My mother continued to defend him and encourage him to beat me after I was returned home. She walked in on him raping me on several occasions and simply turned around and shut the door behind her.

Eventually he did stop beating on my sister and brother and focused his attention on me entirely. I didn't care because I didn't want to see them abused.

I became a chronic runaway. I'd walk the streets all night if I had to. I stopped going to the authorities because they didn't care; at least that's the way it seemed to me. I slept in the woods and on the streets just to get away from that abuse. I used to take my bunny rabbit with me when I ran away, until she died. That was the hardest thing for me to deal with. It seemed worse than the abuse because, finally, something loved me and it was taken away.

To me, the authorities, which were supposed to protect the innocent, actually condoned the behavior of my stepfather. I ran away at least once a week, from age twelve to fifteen. I remember one particular time that I stayed away for three weeks and my family never called the police to look for me.

My stepfather knew that what he was doing was wrong – at least I hoped he knew that. I tried to tell my grandmother, aunts, uncles, cousins, and anyone, who would listen, hoping someone would step forward and try to lend some assistance. Nobody ever did.

I became the black sheep of the family. All everyone ever said was that I was a troublemaker. All I was trying to do was get away from my abusive parents. My life seemed meaningless. I got sick and tired of wanting to die because I wasn't doing anything wrong; he was the problem.

My sister, brother, and I never had an opportunity to bond because I spent so much time running away, trying to get away from my stepfather and mother. I felt bad about our not bonding but I didn't know what else to do. I wished many times I could have taken them with me, but I didn't want to subject them to life on the streets. I didn't know how my life would turn out and I loved them far too much to risk their lives.

Sleeping in the woods and on the streets was no fun. It's not safe and you risk your life every time you do it. You never know whom you might encounter. Then again, with all I was going through, that didn't matter.

Life After the Pain

Chapter 4

Looking for Love in the Wrong Place

Psalm 103:8-9
The Lord is merciful and gracious, slow to anger,
and plentious in mercy.
He will not always chide: neither will he keep his anger forever.

The blood of my Savior paid the price and freed me from any condemnation (John 3:17). My mother took me to abort the baby on February 14, 1983. I was nine weeks pregnant by my stepfather. I sustained a great deal of emotional abuse from him for having the abortion. He wanted me to have the child, but I didn't have a choice in the matter.

He verbally badgered me constantly for about *seven* days about aborting that baby. I was tired of hearing it. The baby was gone and there was nothing I could do to reverse what had been done.

There were times when I felt guilty about aborting the baby; I kept thinking I could have run away and given the baby up for adoption. Then I thought, who would want a baby created in rape? I was too young to know whether I wanted the baby. It was proof of rape, but I didn't want to have a baby just for that reason. It seemed like a cold-hearted reason to bring a child into the world.

I believe that children are a blessing in people's lives, not evidence of rape. I had no voice; I was a minor, and my mother was determined that I wasn't going to bring anymore "havoc" into her home. She probably knew in her heart that I would have tried to run away and have him arrested.

March 15, 1983 I decided I'd taken all I could take of his insults and I ran away. I don't know what was going on in my mind but I ended up in Aberdeen on a strip.

I stopped caring about myself and that's why I ended up on the strip. It's a sad affair but I know that there are other women in society who have felt the same way and done the same thing.

I was tired of being raped over and over again and never protected. I sustained many scars at home, both emotional and physical, and to me nothing on the streets could harm me anymore than what I had already endured. All I ever wanted was the love and support of my mother, but she was emotionally unavailable.

I've learned from many people that what I did was no different than the average adolescent subjected to abuse at home. We are desperate for love and when we don't find it at home, we turn to the streets. All the streets offer are drugs, alcohol, disease, and illicit sex. When we turn to the streets, we run the risk of sustaining more abuse. But to a battered child, the mere possibility of love seems so appealing, and we don't realize the harsh truth of street-life. For me, I was both gullible and naïve; I wanted so badly to be loved that I believed anybody who said they loved me.

As I've stated earlier, abuse has many effects on a person. Some may say that there are no positive effects of abuse, but I must disagree because through every situation I've endured in my life, I've learned a valuable lesson. In addition, each negative situation was bringing me closer to acknowledging the presence of God within! The scripture promises that all things work together for good to them that love God (Romans 8:28), and so it fulfills its purpose in the lives of survivors. For indeed, if we will *"surrender"* our will to His will, we won't have to remain a victim but can consider ourselves victorious in Jesus.

In all, I was on the strip for six days and I'm thankful that God allowed me to be arrested on March 21, 1983 because I could have been killed out there.

I didn't want to ever go back home again but I was on my way back. Once again, against my will and into the hands of the ever present enemy, my stepfather.

The entire ride back home was miserable! He slapped my face for the duration of the drive. He went on and on about how he couldn't believe that I'd given my body away to strangers. He told me that I was his woman and that no woman of his would get away with that. I thought he'd get that gun out and kill me right then and there. I didn't mind, and was indeed hoping that he'd put me out of my misery instantly rather than through a prolonged torture.

The entire ride home he was trying to make me feel guilty about what I had done. He was talking to me like I was a wife who just committed adultery. I thought about trying to jump out of the truck, but then I didn't want to make matters any worse. In my mind, I believed he was going to try to kill me this time and he just might succeed.

Life After the Pain

Chapter 5

Final Brutality

Romans 10:13
*For whosoever shall call upon
the name of the Lord shall be saved.*

$\quad$ I was fifteen-years-old when my stepfather impregnated me. My mother took me to have an exam and confirmed that I was nine weeks pregnant. She immediately arranged for me to have an abortion at Planned Parenthood in Baltimore. She didn't want to have it done near our home in Joppatowne just in case anyone was tracking our family.

$\quad$ Valentine's Day 1983: my nine-week old baby aborted.

$\quad$ Back on the home front, she told my stepfather that I had an abortion. He was furious and slapped her and yelled out, "Why did you kill my baby?" She started crying and said she thought it was the best thing. She expressed her concern that if anyone found out about me being pregnant by him that he might go to jail and she didn't want that to happen. She told him she was trying to protect him. He didn't care about that because all he wanted to know was why she killed his baby? As you see, we're talking about two very sick individuals here, my mother and stepfather. I'm not sure which one is worse, the one beating, or the one *silently* watching?

$\quad$ On March 22, 1983, the next day after my bout with prostitution, my stepfather went out in the woods and cut down a small tree to create a baseball bat. He worked at perfecting that bat for at least two hours. I knew this was going to be the big one: the beating of all beatings!

$\quad$ As I anticipated, he came up to my room and asked me to come downstairs to the family room. I went downstairs at his request, and something inside told me what was about to happen. Somehow, I also knew that it was all about to come to an end, very soon. I simply hoped that if I lived, I'd be able to go on with my life.

$\quad$ My mother, sister, and brother were all in the family room and, for a minute, I thought I might not get a beating after all.

$\quad$ I was wrong. He told me to sit in a chair that was in the middle of the room and then he began beating me with that baseball bat right in front of all of them. He was yelling at the same time that this is what happens when you are disobedient. This is what happens to bad little girls. This is what happens to whores. With every physical strike of the homemade baseball bat against my flesh came a verbal assault. I could feel my flesh burning as I was holding on with all I had to endure this beating. I cried, I screamed, I pleaded for mercy – all to no avail. I believe he struck me over sixty times that evening; there was no part of my body, with the exception of my head, that he didn't hit. God saved me because one good blow to my head and I probably would have died immediately.

I can remember my sister and brother crying. They tried to leave the room, but he wouldn't allow anyone to leave; he made them all watch as he beat me for four straight hours that night. All of my dignity, self-respect, and self-esteem were beat right out of me. I felt completely humiliated because my siblings were forced to witness the verbal and physical abuse.

Afterwards, he picked me up and literally threw me into my bedroom on the floor. I managed to muster up enough strength to get onto my bed where I eventually cried myself to sleep. My hands, arms, legs, buttocks, calves, and feet were bleeding. I was in an extreme amount of pain and I desperately wanted to just go to sleep and die.

As if he had not done enough damage, he came into my room later that night to perform his usual duty of raping me. I couldn't cry or yell for help because my body was numb and still bleeding from the beating earlier. I didn't even want to yell because I knew it would serve no purpose. Mother wasn't going to come to my aid any more now than she had in the past.

The next day, when he came home from work, he yelled upstairs for me to come downstairs. I don't know how I made it downstairs, but I did. As the day before, the family was assembled in the family room and he made me sit in the chair again and began beating me with the baseball bat. The beating went on for at least an hour that night. I tried frantically to get away from the blows because I was still in a tremendous amount of pain from the beating the night before, but my defensiveness only made things worse.

As I sat there, I wondered how a mother could watch her child being brutally beaten and do nothing to protect or defend her. She never cried or showed any signs of compassion toward me.

Afterwards, he raped me right in front of everybody. I was completely numb. I had taken all that I could and I was more than ready to die. And my mother never tried to stop him from the torture that I was facing from that horrifying event of being raped.

On top of all the beatings and rapes that week, he didn't allow my mother to feed me any food and I was locked up in my room like a prisoner. My body was aching for a morsel of nourishment. I felt I was going to die any day from the trauma. The third night, I received more beatings with that baseball bat and I was raped again. These events occurred for six consecutive nights. My body never had the opportunity to start healing before new wounds were added atop the wounds that were already there.

While he was at work, he ordered my mother to watch me so that I didn't try to run away, and she gladly obliged his request. I knew my death was soon approaching. I pleaded with my mother to feed me and save me from what I felt was a slow and miserable death. All she'd say was there was nothing she could do to help me, and that I brought this all on myself.

I felt abandoned by everyone. I knew I was going to die and I wondered whether or not anyone would ever find me, or would my family just bury me in the back yard and claim me as missing?

On the *seventh* day, March 29, 1983 my mother came upstairs to my room and told me that she had to take the kids to school. She'd be right back, she said, and told me not to try anything. Did she actually believe that I wouldn't try to save myself or did God purposely send her out the house so I could have a way of escape? I believe it was the latter of those two possibilities.

Something inside of me told me to call out the name of the Lord for his help. (I now know that was the Holy Spirit speaking to me.) Well, I did exactly that, I cried out, "Lord save me." The Lord heard my cry that morning. I told God that I couldn't take anymore of these beatings, and I wanted a way out of this madness. He used my mother to give me a way out.

I crawled out of the house on my broken knees to find someone who could help. I made it into the arms of a complete stranger, who was standing nearby, and asked her to call the police. The woman, who I had never seen before, did better than that: she drove me to the closest hospital and then notified the police. I never saw her again (an angel strategically placed at the right place at the right moment).

Several physicians examined me that day in Harford Memorial Hospital and it was determined that I had a two broken legs, two broken arms, a hole in my left calf, four broken ribs, a crushed hand/foot, and many contusions that covered my entire body. I was anemic and could no longer fight to heal all the bruises that draped my body like clothing. There wasn't a part of my body that didn't have a bruise, not one part.

The doctors told the police that had I endured one more day of abuse, I would have been **murdered.** I knew I was going to die if I didn't find a way out real soon and then that voice spoke so quietly in my spirit and directed me to call on the Lord.

I cried out, and he heard. My God is awesome!

I will lift up mine eyes unto the hills,
from whence cometh my help.
My help cometh from the Lord,
which made heaven and earth.
Psalm 121:1-2

Approximately nine days after I was admitted to the hospital, I was photographed with all the wounds and bruises that draped my body. The authorities informed me that I'd finally get a conviction because I had sufficient evidence! At last someone believed me, only after death stared me right in the eyes! It didn't matter because I was overjoyed at the fact that I'd never have to go back to that house again.

Let your conversation be without covetousness;
and be content with such things as ye have: for he hath said,
I will never leave thee, nor forsake thee.
So that we may boldly say, The Lord is my helper,
and I will not fear what man shall do unto me.

Life After the Pain

Hebrews 13:5-6

Just as this scripture says, God shall never leave thee nor forsake thee. No matter how bad the situation may seem, God keeps his promises. He will never suffer us to endure more than he knows we can bear (1 Corinthians 10:13). God knew the exact moment to deliver me from that circumstance so in the end He could receive the glory.

A few days after being in the hospital it was determined that I would require emergency surgery performed on my left calf. A splinter from the baseball bat had lodged itself into my leg and the physicians were unable to locate it in order to remove it. Therefore, surgery was necessary in order to avoid amputation because of the amount of infection and swelling that had already found a home in my body. As you can see, God had a plan of his own for my life. Praise the Lord. For the word of the Lord says I shall not die, but live, and declare the works of the Lord (Psalm 118:17).

I was transferred to Johns Hopkins Hospital, located in Baltimore, for the surgery to be performed. After the surgery, during the recovery phase, I remember seeing a bright light when I was under, so bright that I had to cover my eyes. I heard the voice of God, which sounded like thunder as he told me that I had work to do on earth. He said I needed to go back and tell the world what he had done for me. He said I needed to be strong so that one day, at his divine timing, I could tell this story to his people and be a living testimony for someone that *there is life after the pain*. He saved my life and sent me back to earth. He knew back then that I was going to write this book because He is the one who gave me the desire and courage to share my story. The end result is that all things work together for good to them that love God, to them who are the called according to his purpose (Romans 8:28).

Had it been up to me, I never would have shared this story with anyone because I was so ashamed. But it isn't about me; it's about doing God's work, sharing my experiences with abuse so that other's lives may be transformed by my testimony. For God's word states that by the word of our testimony, we can overcome (Revelations 12:11).

Chapter 6

Victory at Last

Hebrews 10:30

For we know him that hath said,
vengeance belongeth unto me,
I will recompense, saith the Lord.
And again, the Lord shall judge his people.

The trial came almost a year later, in January 1984. I remember a very emotional environment. The courtroom was filled with lawyers, news reporters, spectators, my foster parents, and my family.

My mother, sister, and brother were all crying. I tried to tell my mother that I loved her but she yelled at me and said, "I disown you, you're no longer my child, and as far as I'm concerned, you're dead!"

I was angry and hurt, but I had to stay focused on why I was there: thirteen years of abuse, concluding with a brutal and vicious beating which left me with many physical and emotional scars. It was imperative that I continue to pursue what I started: to get him convicted for what he had done to me.

Maybe I was only getting a conviction for that last episode of abuse; but to me, God was gaining victory for all the years of abuse that my stepfather enslaved me to.

I had to take the witness stand and testify. I told the court exactly what I've shared with you. I was cross-examined by my stepfather's attorney, and the only thing he wanted to talk about was the fact that I was arrested for prostitution. He implied that I deserved the vicious beating because I was a prostitute for six days. There is nothing you can do that justifies abuse.

After my testimony there was a recess to give the judge his due time to make a decision. While in the hallway outside the courtroom, my mother hurled hurtful insults at me. She referred to me as a whore, a slut, and whatever else she felt like saying at the time. I didn't respond because I didn't feel the need to disrespect her just because she was being disrespectful toward me.

The newspaper questioned my mother and she told them, "My daughter died." She was referring to me; she promised me that if my stepfather received any jail time, I would be wiped away from her memory completely.

About an hour later, we were called back into the courtroom to receive the judge's decision. The judge gave my stepfather two years of imprisonment and ten years of probation. I remember feeling overjoyed at the victory, for God shined his light in that courtroom. My stepfather was immediately placed under arrest. As he was being escorted away, I remember him looking at me with a sarcastic smile. It wasn't a smile of regret; it was a smile that said to me, "Oh well, I finally got caught." I looked back at him, shook my head, and left the courtroom.

Outside the courtroom several reporters waited to capture any last comments from either side. I was asked how I felt about the outcome of the trial and I responded with a smile: "I can't say how happy I am, I really think justice was done." I added, "I feel safer now, and I know that he'll suffer for what he did to me." The last comment I made before leaving the courthouse was, "Praise the Lord, life goes on."

That was it for me, that chapter of my life closed, and I knew he would never be able to abuse me again. Praise the Lord.

Under Maryland law, my stepfather could have received up to fifteen years for the child abuse conviction. Had he been found guilty of the other charges that were dropped, he could have additionally been sentenced to not more than twenty years for second degree rape, two to fifteen years for assault with intent to rape, plus two to ten more years for assault and battery. The "good" judicial system of this society dropped all those charges against him and the state's attorney accepted a plea bargain without any consultation with me. How pathetic.

I found out that the State's Attorney and the Judge were up for re-election that year. I wonder if that had anything to do with the verdict? Anyhow, at least he ended up with some time because, to me, some was better than none.

Originally, the lawyer for my stepfather wanted the charges dropped completely and the State's Attorney tried to persuade me to drop the charges against my stepfather and leave the case alone. I declined that offer and insisted the case go to trial.

April 19, 1984 the attorney for my stepfather actually went back to the judge to ask for a shorter sentence. The lawyer stated that my stepfather had made a successful adjustment at the Harford County Detention Center. He extended his comment to say that my stepfather had even been allowed to work outside the center at the Sheriff's Department and the Bel Air Police Department. The lawyer stated that my stepfather had always been a productive member of society and that his family needed him back at home.

Now, let me ask you, as the reader of this book, how does that sound? A convicted rapist/child abuser is allowed to work in your local police district? What kind of sign does that send out to abusers? It seems as though the actions of the abuser are being condoned.

I went to the Bel Air Police Department in the summer of 1997 to read my stepfather's statements, the ones taken by the authorities on March 31, 1983. I was curious about what exactly he had to say for himself.

His entire statement was a big lie! He admitted to beating me on March 22, 1983 and he said that he only struck me four times. LIE! He stated that when he brought me home from the police station after being arrested for prostitution that he threatened to kill me and I in turn offered to have sex with him. LIE! He went on to say that he began to beat me with the baseball bat that he made until I started yelling for the Lord to save me. He then claimed that he stopped hitting me. LIE!

Before he was advised of his rights, the last thing he stated was that I deserved what I got; he only did what was right. The police stopped him, advised him of his rights, and he waived his rights. Now here's the killer: he wasn't placed under arrest that day. He was allowed to leave and go home. He wasn't officially arrested until April 15, 1983 at 8:30 p.m., nearly two weeks after the incidents occurred. Now that's what I call efficiency.

At the very end of the ordeal, the AEGIS paper interviewed me for a follow-up story about my newfound life after the abuse. I was asked how I had been since the trial. I responded, "I'm doing fine and I've since given my life to God, am going to church with my new foster family, and doing very well in school." I further stated that I had given my life to Jesus Christ on October 23, 1983, and since that time my life had changed dramatically.

After the trial I went back to living with my foster family in Darlington. However, soon after the trial, my foster-mother started drinking excessively and I was subsequently removed from the home.

I was sent to Baltimore to live in a group home named Jane Egenton Home, along with *seven* other girls who had also sustained some form of abuse. I went to Southern High School, joined the school band, Jr. ROTC training, and was an honor roll student. I graduated in 1985 with a 98.2% overall average. It was obviously the hand of God that rested gently upon my life.

Life in the Jane Egenton Home was very good. I don't have a lot of memories of living there but what I have chosen to remember are all fond remembrances of some very nice ladies who worked there, and I'd like to take this opportunity to thank for their invaluable contribution to my life. Their names, which I hope they won't mind me giving honorable mention, are Ms. Jones, Mrs. Humes, Mrs. Walker, Ms. Hilton, and Mrs. Jenkins. They may never know, full extent of the *positive* impact they left upon my heart and life. May God richly bless each one, wherever they may be in life. And, I'd also like to mention a few of the young ladies who also stayed there, who also played a *positive* role in my life, even in the midst of their storm. Their names are: Yolanda, Linda, Sandy, Doreen, Veronica, and Tee-Tee. I don't have contact with any of them, but I pray wherever they may be that they are equally as blessed.

I moved out of the group home into my own apartment when I was seventeen years old. I survived all those years of abuse with a testimony of victory, Praise the Lord.

I want to thank the Lord for his deliverance in my life concerning the abuse I sustained for the last fifteen years of my life. Truly God is able to do all things if we only believe (Mark 9:23).

Life After the Pain

Chapter 7

No Idea

---

1 Corinthians 10:13
There hath no temptation taken you
but such as is common to man:
but God is faithful,
who will not suffer you to be tempted
above that ye are able;
but will with the temptation
also make a way to escape,
that ye may be able to bear it.

I could still hear my mother's voice saying, "You'll never amount to anything." Needless to say, I didn't go on to college after graduating from high school on June 12, 1985. I guess that was hard enough for me to accomplish, given my past.

In the summer of 1986, almost a year after moving out of the group home, I met the man who would become my husband.

Soon after our meeting, approximately three months, we decided to move in together. I was almost eighteen years old and it seemed like a good idea. Sometime between the time I left the group home and the time that I met him, I had stopped going to church.

I'm aware now that because I was physically involved with this man, my spiritual life suffered. It didn't have to be that way; it was a choice I made subconsciously.

I believe that the Lord sent this man into my life to teach me a few lessons I desperately needed to learn. Reality set in at thirty-one years of age and permitted me to face the fact that this was a situation that I chose to be involved, not one I was forced into. For so long I believed that in order to serve God, I had to abide by certain guidelines. And, if I found myself falling short according to man's standards, I turned my back on God, thinking that I was unworthy.

I did eventually pursue a relationship with God after my boyfriend and I were married, believing I would be at least somewhat worthy of God's love now.

While I was pursuing biblical studies, my husband was pursuing the world. He became heavily involved in drug dealing. I kept praying he would someday surrender his life to God, but it never happened. I wanted my marriage to work, but it just seemed inevitable that it would fail, in my own mind.

Aside from our opposite beliefs, we did share many happy times together. He was a peaceful and happy man, willing to go the extra mile to help anyone. I just recognize today that we were at different stages in our lives and I have come to peace with that.

My husband ended up being sentenced to five years imprisonment for drug dealing. Prior to his arrest, I finally decided to leave, I just was unwilling to play second to the life he pursued on the streets. And, for me it was the best thing to do.

Sometimes in life we make poor choices and get involved in relationships for the wrong reasons. Perhaps he and I became involved to teach each other a few lessons, and that makes it all worthwhile.

Life After the Pain

Chapter 8

Time to Pick Up the Pieces

Isaiah 40:31
*But they that wait upon the Lord
shall renew their strength;
they shall mount up with wings as eagles;
they shall run, and not be weary;
and they shall walk, and not faint.*

After leaving my husband, I began to pick up the broken pieces of my life, to put them back together again. I once again stopped going to church. I formulated the belief in my mind that God had left me because of my failed marriage. And, quite honestly, I didn't see any need in continuing to pursue bible studies to learn of a God who left me when I needed him the most.

Today I recognize that it was merely a way of God getting my attention away from the religious doctrine I was studying at the time. Yes, a marriage was sacrificed in the process but God knew what was best for us.

Sometime during the course of his incarceration, my ex-husband surrendered his life to God. And, is doing very well today, so God definitely worked things for the good in his life.

As for me, I chose to remain single to give myself needed time to grieve the loss of my ex-husband. When I agreed to marry him, I hoped it would last a lifetime. I had a major adjustment to make because I went from being married and believing in forever, to being single and separated from my husband.

I did meet someone whom I eventually entered into a relationship with for almost three years. I got that divorce and was actually going to marry this gentleman. Something on the inside, however, would not allow me to move in that direction. That something down on the inside is known as the Holy Spirit. I know that today. Even though I thought God had left me, in fact, he hadn't.

The relationship with this man was very similar to the one with my ex-husband. He had no desire for spiritual growth and I kept longing for the Lord; I went to church occasionally but never for long. My mind kept telling me that I couldn't have a relationship with God, as though I was unclean.

No matter how many tricks my mind tried to play on me, I never stopped praying. I kept a prayer journal for years in which I would write love letters to God, about how I wanted to develop a relationship with him. I wanted to be delivered from all the pain I'd experienced and from the obvious bondage I had myself in because of the past. I knew my help was on the way; I just didn't know when or how. Today, I acknowledge the fact that I don't need to know how; all I need to do is trust God.

This relationship was not good for me and the Holy Spirit kept trying to awaken me from my carnal sleep, so I could leave, but I refused to listen. I thought that man loved me and that's all I wanted, to be loved.

I kept searching for love, but I now know I was looking for love in all the *wrong* places. I identified love as abuse, and the more someone abused me, the more I thought he loved me. That is part of the sickness that abuse victims are left with.

I packed my things and left because I had taken all I could of his mental abuse and cheating. I just moved out, and it was the best thing I could have done for the both of us. It gave us both the much-needed opportunities for growth and maturity. We did maintain a friendship and got along better as friends than we did in a relationship.

So again, all things do work together for good to those who love God (Romans 8:28). That has become one of my favorite scriptures because it lets us know that no matter what happens in our lives, God has a plan and he will turn it around for our good according to *His* purpose.

Life After the Pain

Chapter 9

No Need to Run

Matthew 11:28
Come unto me,
all ye that labour and are heavy laden,
and I will give you rest.

We all make mistakes and have sordid pasts. God did not send Jesus into the world to condemn the world (us); but that the world through him might be saved (John 3:17).

I have done many things in my life that I used to regret. But I know there were some things I did that were a part of God's plan for my life. I lived many years below my means, simply meaning that I lived a very promiscuous life. Running from one relationship to another, looking for someone to fill the emptiness that I felt inside, I was ignorant of the fact that what I was searching for was not in someone else, but was living inside of me the entire time: God.

God didn't condemn me in the midst of my past, but he loved me in spite of it. He loved me with an everlasting love: therefore with loving kindness he has drawn me to himself (Jeremiah 31:3). For I did not choose God, but he chose me, and ordained me that I may go and bring forth fruit (John 15:16). Praise God.

I have learned many things as I look back over my life, filled with one broken relationship after another. The most important lesson I learned was how to love myself. That may seem easy, but to a person whose life has been filled with abuse, it's sometimes very hard. It's difficult because we continue to look for love in the wrong places. We search for happiness in others instead of within ourselves. The truth is you must first be happy with yourself or you will find misery always on your doorstep.

A companion is only there to enhance your happiness. It is not their responsibility to "make" you happy or feel good. There must be contentment with self.

The second thing I had to face was that I lacked self-respect. Obviously, if you don't love something or someone, you won't feel respect either. Do you batter something or someone you love? I don't think you would.

In order for me to develop self love and respect I had to change people, places, and things in my life. I had to change the group of people I chose to associate with as friends. I had to change the places I used to go because it wasn't conducive to the relationship I was trying to develop with God. Finally, I had to change quite a few things I used to do, such as drinking, smoking, cursing, and clubbing. I desperately had to learn how to be obedient to what I knew was right for me.

I chose to stop those former actions because they didn't work for me. I can't live my life according to what seems to work for everyone else. I must be true to myself and do what is best for me. I won't allow someone else to dictate what is right or wrong for my life. I do have the godly wisdom within to make both an intelligent and competent decision concerning my life.

I have found that what works for you may not work for me and vice versa. No two people can follow the same advice, the same exact way, because we were all created differently. In the same image, but yet so different. The great part is that it's okay to be different, it doesn't make us bad people because we may disagree on any given matter.

I have met many people who tried to beat and whip me with the word of God. They used his word to manipulate and influence me into doing what they wanted me to do. My love for God was used as a weakness, and I'm sure it has been for many others, and that's known as spiritual abuse.

Yes, I have made some poor decisions in life, but it doesn't lessen God's love for me. *He accepts me just as I am and he will accept you too because he is no respecter of person* (Acts 10:34).

As a song I heard says, "What God has for you, it is for you." Nothing is going to stop God's plan for your life or mine. He knows what he has for your life, plans for peace and not evil (Jeremiah 29:11). Many times when bad things happen people like to blame the "devil" but I'm here to tell you that everything bad that happens isn't the "devil's" fault. Many things you bring on yourself; as the word of God says, "You reap what you sow" (Galatians 6:7). Stop blaming the so-called devil and instead start taking responsibility for your contribution to the confusion you've allowed to entangle you!

I am not a judge or one to condemn. We must learn how to sweep around our own house before we try to sweep around someone else's house. These are the words of a very old song. Praise God because someone knew what he was singing about. Even the word teaches us to get the log out of our eye before we try to take the speck out of our brother's eye (Matthew 7:3).

I shared this portion of my testimony because God said there are a lot of people, both men and women, who can relate to and understand what I experienced. He also wants you to know that we don't have to stay in abusive relationships just for the sake of having someone. He has not called us to be anybody's doormat and it's time for us to stand up and say, "Enough is enough!"

I am not a whipping post nor am I someone you use, abuse, and throw away like yesterday's garbage. I am the ***daughter of God*** and I demand respect. You see, the greatest thing I learned from living below my means was not only who I wasn't, but more importantly, who *I* am! Praise God.

Chapter 10

Don't Minimize My Pain

Psalm 52:8
*But I am like a green olive tree
in the house of God:
I trust in the mercy of God for ever and ever.*

One thing that anyone who has ever been abused in any shape, form, or fashion has in common is the inability to trust. It's not something we automatically give after being violated; trust must be earned is what we quickly learn.

All too often I hear someone telling a survivor to just "get over it" and move on. Please be mindful in saying that to a victim or survivor because abuse is not something you just get over. With time and patience, we learn three things in recovering from the effects of abuse, and they are that we don't get over whatever may have happened to us, we learn to get: around it, past it, and through it.

It can seem to be a very lengthy process in the beginning, but, nonetheless, it is possible. For we know that because we are the children of God, that all things are possible to him that believes (Mark 9:23). All we need to do is believe it in our hearts and in our minds and so it shall be. The word of God teaches us that as a person thinks in his heart, so is he (Proverbs 23:7). We must recognize that we have the power within to determine the outcome of our future.

If you think negatively, negativity will come to you, and if you think positively, then positivity will come to you. If you look at yourself as a victim, then you will always be someone's victim, but if you would spend that time believing that you are a survivor, you shall become more than a conqueror. You will begin to see the reality of a promise given to you from God, that in all things we are more than conquerors through him that loved us (Romans 8:37), and that nothing shall be able to separate you from the love of God (Romans 8:39), nothing at all. Praise God! That is definitely something to be excited about!

From my own personal experience with trust challenges, I know that it is very difficult. Especially when you find it in your heart to trust someone again after being hurt, and s/he hurts you all over again. That happens most often in our relationships, our partner does something to break our trust (i.e. lying, talking behind our back, infidelity), then s/he may apologize and ask for another chance. Eventually, we may agree to give the relationship another try. Often times, we find ourselves repeatedly faced with the same situation or circumstance. Then, we whip ourselves with thoughts such as, "I didn't use any wisdom, I should have known better, or I knew he hadn't changed."

The reality of the matter is that we knew, if we are completely honest with ourselves, that the person hadn't changed. The reason, at least one of the main reasons, we keep going back to those old relationships is because we are working out issues from our past abuse. Until we are prepared to face the fact that we need to heal and break away from those relationships, we will keep repeating the same cycle, over and over and over again.

Relationships sometimes appear to be the root cause of our challenge to trust. However, I don't entirely agree with the theory because based on my abuse as a child from my parents, it became inevitable that I would also face that challenge of trust in my adult life.

Psychologists say that by the time you are five or six years of age, you have already established how you will think in your future. Now if that is true, if you spent those years being abused by the same people you were supposed to look to for love, then how would you feel? Probably not very good. However, based on that information, be it true or not, you would have grown up believing you couldn't trust anyone. In other words, what must now take place is you must retrain your thinking, begin to replace all those negative messages with positive ones.

I always say that I don't need anyone to affirm who I am, because I am very confident of who exactly I am! I have taken on some positive affirmations and I repeatedly remind myself of a few simple statements. I am going to recommend a few to you and suggest that you try speaking them into and over your life and watch the changes that will begin to take place. Here are a few:

1. I am loveable and I am loved.
2. I am at peace within and I radiate peace wherever I am.
3. I am trustworthy and I am trusting.
4. I am special and I accept compliments from others.
5. I was created for a purpose, I accept it, and I walk in it daily.

Take some time right now and repeat each one of the statements five times. Then I want you to sit still and receive the blessings of peace!

You don't have to sit around and wait for someone else to encourage you, encourage yourself! That is the assignment of positive affirmations. You can write those affirmations down on a separate sheet of paper and take some time everyday to repeat them and watch the changes that begin to take place in your life.

Be patient with yourself: it will take time to come to the place where you will be able to trust. I know for me, sometimes it was hard to trust God because I didn't know if He would hurt me the way others had hurt me in the past. I'm pleased to say that I have put my total trust in God and He has never hurt me, not one time. In fact, his word promises you and I that his thoughts of us are always good and not evil (Jeremiah 29:11). Isn't that great news? A loving Father who loves us, cares for us, and who thinks about our future well-being. That sure makes me feel good to know that no matter what challenge I may be faced with in life, God knows all about it.

Rest assured, even as the scripture reference (Psalm 52:8) for this chapter assures us, we can trust in the mercy of God. My point being that if we don't always trust the way we want to, act the way we'd like to, or say the things we desire to, God's mercy is unchanging.

One day at a time, one hour at a time, one minute at a time, and sometimes one second at a time I will begin to practice trusting. And, if someone fails and breaks my trust, I will forgive, and keep in mind that I sometimes fail, too. But, we now have another chance to make it right and correct our mistakes.

With that, go forth in peace and know that the fervent prayers of the righteous do avail much (James 5:16). If nobody has said so lately, allow me to say, "I love you in Jesus' name."

God richly bless!

Chapter 11

Sweet Spirit of a Loving Sister

Matthew 7:7-8

Ask, and it shall be given you;
seek, and ye shall find;
knock, and it shall be opened unto you:
For every one that asketh receiveth;
and he that seeketh findeth;
and to him that knocketh it shall be opened.

Life After the Pain

When you least expect it, something you've been believing in God for will come to pass. I prayed for many years that a day would come when I would be able to see my sister, brother, and niece. Because of the abuse I sustained as a child and the denial which my mother continues to cling to, I am denied visitation with my siblings.

The Lord arranged for me to cross paths with the best friend of my sister. We engaged in a lengthy conversation and concluded with the exchange of telephone numbers and a verbal agreement to meet via telephone.

Within *three* days, I received a telephone call and had the privilege of speaking with my sister, whom I hadn't spoke to in over three years. It was a most equally uplifting event. Soon thereafter, the Lord allowed my sister to win a trip to California. She was being forced to take my brother with her, but I made separate travel arrangements through the grace of God, so I could meet them there.

Truly I thank and praise my Lord and Savior for the opportunity to spend three days with my siblings away from our parents. We all managed to keep it hidden and nobody ever knew that I was there with them. For the rest of my life, I will cherish the memories I have from that trip.

The Lord made provisions on our behalf so that we could see one another every weekend over the course of approximately *seven* months. We were permitted by the grace of God to share Christmas, New Year's, Valentine's Day, and both of their birthdays together before the eventual separation.

It was *seven* months of love, joy, and peace shared among us. My sister and I were talking on the telephone nearly every night and bonding the way God originally intended for us. She would ask for advice and wisdom on matters of life because I am eight years older, and it made me feel great.

My sister has a loving spirit filled with the agape love of God. She is a very tender hearted and compassionate young woman. I believe, if anything, my sister was praying for me. My sister knew of my sordid past and never made any judgements against me at all.

62

It's important for us to see what the Lord was allowing to take place. My sister was being used by God to come into darkness and let the light of Jesus shine before me that I would come to glorify Jesus (Matthew 5:16). The bible states that God will bring to light the hidden things of darkness (1 Corinthians 4:5).

I'm thankful for the obedience of my sister to the gospel of Jesus Christ. She didn't plant seeds of hatred toward me because my lifestyle caused me to turn to God with love. I reflect on this scripture, when I think of her, found in 1 John 4:7: *Beloved, let us love one another; for love is of God; and every one that loveth is born of God, and knoweth God.* Indeed, she is a woman of God filled with the integrity and wisdom that a woman should display toward a sister who didn't recognize God as the only power within.

I'm also thankful for the love my brother displayed toward me. He is an ambitious young man filled with dreams and visions for the future. When I think of him, I reflect upon Acts 2:17: *And it shall come to pass in the last days, saith God, I will pour out my spirit upon all flesh; and your sons and daughters shall prophesy, and your young men shall see visions, and your old men shall dream dreams.*

Both my sister and brother have been blessed with a college education and are successful, business-minded individuals, but Christ is their head.

The more love I received from my sister and brother, the more I wanted. In my fury one day, I called my mother to tell her that my siblings and I had been communicating and I didn't want to sneak around anymore.

I realize today that it wasn't anybody's fault but my own for our separation. I wanted desperately for my sister and brother to stand up to our parents and admit their love for me and desire to be a part of my life, but they were entertaining the spirit of fear. Instead of praying and asking for God's will, I decided to take matters into my own hands.

The end result is I haven't seen or heard from my sister or brother since April, 1998. Yes, it hurts, but I'm learning to accept the responsibility of allowing my own thoughts to control me. I wish I had the spiritual knowledge then that I have today.

Again, I must say indeed all things do work together for good to them that love God (Romans 8:28) and I will certainly love the Lord and seek to do his will, in spite of this challenge.

I went on a *three* day fast and closed myself off from all outside communication in February of 1999. I was in search of precise answers from God on some issues of importance to me. One of the issues was concerning my family and why I'm rejected and cast out. The Lord spoke so sweetly and said to me, *"They're not rejecting you my child, they're rejecting the God who lives in you."* I can't tell you how invigorating that release was for me. It was all I needed to hear on the matter. God knew exactly what I needed because I had dealt with that spirit of rejection by my family for many years.

Well, it didn't stop there. Since picking up my cross and deciding to recognize God within, many folks have decided not to associate with me anymore. Once again, the Lord spoke so softly on May 26, 1999 the same thing he spoke during my shut-in, but this time he backed it up with his word. He took me right to the scripture found in Luke 10:16 which states, *He that heareth you heareth me; and he that despiseth me despiseth him that sent me.* The word "despiseth" in many translated versions of the bible means rejected.

Therefore, I thank and praise God for my deliverance over this matter. I still miss my family and desire for them to be a part of my life, but they are not God, nor do they have the last word on the matter. Let it not be my will, but thine, be done (Luke 22:42).

Chapter 12

Telling the Truth vs. Telling a Lie

John 8:32
And ye shall know the truth,
and the truth shall make you free.

The truth will always make you free. God is a God who cannot lie (Titus 1:2). Christ suffered for us, leaving us an example, that we should follow his steps (1 Peter 2:21). So if we are to follow his steps and God cannot lie, then neither should we.

For me this was a very hard struggle for many years after being delivered from the abuse. For years, I had told the truth and cried out for help and nobody responded. It left such a bitter taste in my mouth that I began to lie when I became an adult. I told people whatever I thought they wanted to hear, and that wasn't good for them or me.

It led me into a life filled with deceit because I was too embarrassed to say I had been raped. I entertained the spirit of fear for years because I didn't think people would like me if they knew all about my past. But God has not given me the spirit of fear; he has given me power, love, and a sound mind (2 Timothy 1:7). When we operate in the spirit God has given unto us we will not entertain the spirit of fear any longer. If we stand up and submit ourselves to God, he will bless our efforts to live right.

He that speaks lies shall perish (Proverbs 19:9); the word of God is clear and concise in its warnings against lies. The purpose of this book is for God to minister to the hearts and minds of the readers to begin a transformation. If there is anything in you that is not like God, I pray he will purge it out so that he may begin to use you according to his will and plan for your life.

For we were born, not of blood, nor of the will of the flesh, nor of the will of man, but of God (John 1:13). We must keep in mind that we were sent to earth to fulfill a purpose. God has a purpose for each one of us to fulfill. Never compromise the word of God. Learn to rightly divide the word for your personal understanding. Ask the Lord for all you need because his word assures us that if we ask, we shall receive (Matthew 7:7). The only reason we have not is because we ask not (James 4:2).

Chapter 13

Faith to Move a Mountain

---

1 Peter 1:8-9
Whom having not seen, ye love;
in whom, though now ye see him not, yet believing,
ye rejoice with joy unspeakable and full of glory:
Receiving the end of your faith, even the salvation of your souls.

Faith.

A word we tend to take lightly, but I believe it is faith which carries us through the many trials of our lives.

Faith is the substance of things hoped for and the evidence of things not seen (Hebrews 11:1). I interpret that scripture in that I say my prayers asking for all I need God to move on, and believe it shall come to pass, thereby being the evidence. I can't actually see God moving on the prayer but my faith assures me that he will. No prayer goes unheard.

God tells us in his word that if we have faith as small as a mustard seed that we can say "move" to a mountain and it shall move; nothing is impossible for us (Matthew 17:20). All we have to do is believe, (have faith), and all things become possible (Mark 9:23).

One night while in prayer and meditation, God revealed Jeremiah 32:27 which states: *Behold, I am the Lord, the God of all flesh, Is there anything too hard for me?* That scripture began to minister to my level of faith. Every time I think about where God has brought me from, I realize there is nothing too hard for him.

I have begun a process of taking every single thing to him in prayer, no matter how small, and it works. Let me share a testimony with you that shows God is even concerned about the little things in our lives, no matter how small they may seem to us.

I was packing to go away on vacation and I realized I didn't have any tennis shoes that were decent enough to take along with me. I began to talk with Jesus about the matter and I told him that I really didn't have the money to buy any but I sure would love to have a new pair if he desired me to have a pair. I continued packing and left that matter in prayer.

The next day, while I was at work, my sister in the Lord called and told me to stop by her house on my way home because she had a brand new pair of tennis shoes for me. I asked her how much I owed her and she said nothing, and that the Lord laid it on her heart to bless me. She had no idea what I asked God for but God knew and answered my prayer!

God is concerned about everything in your life. No matter how big or small, take it to the Lord in prayer and I guarantee he will answer.

There is only one answer from God concerning our prayers and that is always yes. His desire is for us to live a healthy, happy, and prosperous life. He designed us and knows every hair on our heads for each are numbered (Matthew 10:30). When I read that scripture it shows me just another aspect of our creator: think about how many of our hairs fall out on a daily basis, but yet, he knows the very number at any appointed time, thank you God. That's a father who knows his children.

I recommend that you start keeping a prayer journal. If you want to increase your faith, take some time to write in a prayer journal. It will do many things for you that you never could have imagined.

My prayer journal gives me the peace that passes all understanding because when I sit down with my pen and paper, I'm coming to give it *all* to God. I begin by thanking him for the opportunity and then I express my gratitude for all the things God did for me that day. And, I conclude with writing a positive affirmation that I can meditate as I linger off to sleep. My prayer journal gives me privilege of considering others before making prayers for myself. It gives me the opportunity to be quiet before the Lord and sometimes he'll even use my hand to write the answer back to me. The best part of a prayer journal is the leisure of being able to go back and read it and see how many of my prayers God answered. Now that's a powerful faith builder when you know for yourself that the prayers of the righteous are heard by God (Proverbs 15:29).

We must anchor our faith on the unchanging, everlasting Lord, whose promises never fail and whose love is all encompassing. Our joy and hope can be as unwavering as the sunrise even when the happenings around us are transitioning from superb to disastrous. Scripture teaches us that His peace is there for those who choose to take it (2 Thessalonians 3:16). So I say stand in faith and know your blessing is within, waiting for you to recognize it.

Life After the Pain

Chapter 14

Deliverance from a Wicked Past

Romans 8:38
For I am persuaded, that neither death,
nor life, nor angels, nor principalities,
nor powers, nor things present, nor things to come,
nor height, nor depth, nor any other creature
shall be able to separate us from the love of God,
which is in Christ Jesus our Lord.

Life After the Pain

In the Bible, in the book of Isaiah 55:11, God speaks of his word not returning void; what he pleases shall be accomplished. God isn't the author of confusion but of peace (1 Corinthians 14:33).

Therefore it would be accurate to say that God is more than able to deliver us from the hurt of our past. As the scripture for this chapter recites in detail, nothing shall be able to separate us from the love of God, which is in Christ Jesus. Absolutely nothing and nobody!

Each piece that I've written about my life symbolizes that I've been delivered time after time from my childhood into my adulthood. God has been good to me; I know that beyond a shadow of doubt and I don't take that for granted.

Just because things happen to us that are bad doesn't mean that something good can't or won't come out of it. It may seem strange to the average person to hear me say this, but I'm extremely thankful for each experience I've lived through.

The key for me is exactly that – I survived! I've learned that sometimes it's not life or love that's bad, per se, it's us making it bad with our thoughts about any given situation or circumstance.

That means God blessed me with his mercy and grace and I'm going to take my experiences in stride. You can take each bad experience and turn it into a powerful teaching tool. However, I do want you to know that I didn't recognize the good things that came from my experiences until after the age of thirty, so don't worry if you aren't at this stage yet in life. Be patient, it shall come to pass. The first step in making it happen is recognizing a need for change.

From most of the experiences I endured, I learned that a complete and total dependency upon God will take you a long way!

My childhood years were difficult, filled with tears and an enormous amount of pain. But God delivered me, and I learned that, despite the situation, weeping may endure for a night but joy will *always* greet you the next morning (Psalm 30:5). I learned from the scripture that a night in God's vision isn't always what we know as night. God is not limited by time as we are, so a night may be a long season but joy will

72

come. Each and every time I've spent the night crying, I've always experienced abundant joy shortly thereafter.

It may seem incredulous, and even I find it hard to believe, but I learned a lot from my mother, things that I'll cherish the rest of my life. I want to first say *I love my mother* very much. Despite the past, the fact remains that she's my mother and I'll always love her, no matter what. For the word of God says to honor our father and mother that our days may be long (Exodus 20:12).

The biggest thing I learned from my mother is how to be economical. My mother also taught me how to keep a clean house, and be a good cook. From the years of neglect from her, I learned to depend on God for all things. That probably was the greatest lesson of all because when she was emotionally unavailable, God stepped in and took her place. For the word of God says when my father and mother forsake me, he will take me in (Psalm 27:10). I know my mother loves me in her own way and I hope that one day I'll be able to write a sequel to this book and tell you that we've developed a relationship. Some may say it's unlikely, but there's nothing wrong with having faith. And, we know with God, all things are possible, even a reconciliation.

From my stepfather I learned the type of men I don't want in my life. I also learned the type of person that I am. I would never allow anyone to abuse my child and keep that person in my life. No man is worth that much. There isn't any excuse that will suffice in my mind because I've lived it. I'm thankful because I wouldn't be the woman that I am today had it not been for the experience. I've learned to look beyond the outer surface of circumstances and look within to find a little piece of beauty in all longsuffering. I even learned to look within and find the beauty of God that loves within my stepfather.

I've become a very strong person and I thank God that I'm able to write this book and testify that I survived. I wasn't consumed by the circumstances and am now able to give God the glory for delivering me.

From the experience of prostitution I learned many things, most importantly that two wrongs don't make a right. Just because my stepfather was raping me didn't mean that I had to go out on the streets and sell my body. Praise God for he kept me even in the midst of that storm. Most importantly, I learned I am much better than the experience of rape.

The last thing I learned was that none of us are superior to others. People sometimes walk around like they are better than others are but I realized that we're all created alike in the eyes of God. God is no respecter of persons (Acts 10:34). No matter how big your house may be, what kind of car you drive, what kind of job you hold, how much money you make, or how many businesses you own, you are no better than anybody else!

Remember all those things are superficial and will not get you into the gates of Heaven. I know because I used to believe that all those things made me better than others; however, today, I believe it is because of the Christ that lives within that I am special, and it makes you special, too.

In my former marriage, I learned quite a few things that I'm still applying in my life now. Everything that looks good on the outside isn't always good for you. He was a good man; we were just too young. I also learned that for every way in, there's always a way out, for God will always make a way of escape (1 Corinthians 10:13).

From my promiscuous lifestyle, I learned more things than I sometimes care to admit. The first thing I learned is that I should have had more self-respect; I had the wisdom of God to practice and I wish I would have used it. However, that's what life is about, learning from our mistakes. I appreciate that the Lord brought me through that lifestyle victorious, and that it didn't take twenty years. And, I am not regretful of my past because it played a vital part in my needed growth.

I learned one thing of incredible value and that was to stand on my own. I learned that I don't require a man for survival. The only man I need for survival is Jesus Christ. Believe it or not, I'm closer to God now more than I've ever been. Sometimes we have to drop to rock bottom in order for our eyes to open up, and that's exactly what happened to me. I had to have the bottom fall out, and then I learned how to find comfort in solitude. Praise God!

I'm learning daily to simply "let go and let God." I assure you that each time I've humbled myself and given him control of any situation, he has *never* failed me. Deliverance is a mighty powerful force blessed by God. That may be the best lesson I learned from being a promiscuous woman. It all comes back to "all things are possible through God if we believe" (Mark 9:23).

By always telling the truth instead of telling a lie, one can learn a great deal. I learned that telling the truth will indeed set you free (John 8:32). The only thing I ever lied about in my childhood was being a prostitute for six days. Many people still don't know the truth about that, but now this book exposes that secret and my, how I feel free!

My mother, for many years, even to this day, believes that I lied about her husband raping me. I pray that someday she will be blessed with the gift of reality! It is hard to tell the truth to someone when it is not what she wants to hear. In the society we live in today, I recommend that we all tell now rather than be found out later.

Something else I learned was to never underestimate my initial feelings (i.e.: Holy Spirit, intuition, gut reaction). If something doesn't feel right, let it go. I spent far too many years wishing I had used my first instincts on situations. I made a lot of mistakes and despite the fact that today I am a born again, baptized, holy ghost-filled Christian woman, I sometimes still make mistakes, but now I know how to get back up and try again.

From the reunion with my siblings, I learned that I'll never take any moment spent with them for granted. Remember to always let the ones you love know how much they mean to you. For we never know what tomorrow holds; you truly may never see that person again. And if that happens, you're left with regrets and wishes of what you could have said or done. Someone once told me that wishes are simply "wasted energy" and he was absolutely correct. The most valuable lesson I learned was that if you pray for something, God does hear and will answer. I prayed for many years for the opportunity to spend time with my siblings and, when I least expected it, God brought them forth. I praise the Lord for the time and I patiently await the day when we're joined together again. This time I'm praying that nothing and nobody will be able to separate us.

From my challenges with trust, I learned to continue to cast all my cares upon God, because He cares for me. I have learned to stand on the scripture that promises me that no weapon formed against me shall prosper (Isaiah 54:17). So, even if my trust is violated, I can forgive and accept the fact, that I, too, fail sometimes in life. Again, all things do work together for the good to them that love God. We must keep pressing on, no matter how hard it may seem, for we do have the power wtihin.

Deliverance can come in many forms. It will appear as a removal from a bad situation, and as a transformation from a previous way of living. Deliverance will give you a new way of thinking, acting, walking, talking, and dressing. For when the spirit of the Lord is upon you, you can do nothing but change your ways entirely. The Holy Spirit causes me to search out the word of God every day that he has blessed me with life. It causes me to seek God in prayer at work, home, and even in my car. I try not to do anything today unless I pray about it first and feel led by the Holy Spirit to carry out his will.

Deliverance has taught me many valuable lessons that I will cherish for the rest of my life.

Chapter 15

Divine Friendship

John 15:12-13
This is my commandment,
That ye love one another,
as I have loved you.
Greater love hath no man than this,
that a man lay down his life for his friends.

Friendship is a subject some may think doesn't merit serious
discussion. On the contrary, it must be brought in from the darkness
where it currently resides.

First, I want you to know that it's the will of God for us to have
friendships with others. However, it's not his will for us to have
friendships at all costs. It's not his will for us to compromise our morals
or beliefs just for the sake of having a friend in our lives. For the word of
God tells us that to be a friend of the world is to be the enemy of God
(James 4:4).

My personal experience with friendships has varied. Before I get
into the kind of friendships I've had, however, I want to share with you
the story of a friend who will stick closer than a brother and his name is
Jesus Christ (Proverbs 18:24).

Every good gift and every perfect gift is from above, from our
father in heaven because he loves us (James 1:17). God loved us so much
that he sent his only son to die for us (John 3:16). I believe that was an
awesome act of love for his people. It wasn't that we loved God; it was
that he loved us.

I don't believe anybody walking this earth can say they have a
friend more awesome than God. I'm thankful that he's my friend and
that he considers me a friend.

*Greater love hath no man than this, that a man lay down his life for his
friends. Ye are my friends, if ye do whatever I command you. Henceforth I call you
not servants; for the servant knoweth not what his lord doeth; but I have called you
friends; for all things that I have heard of my Father I have made known unto you.
Ye have not chosen me, but I have chosen you, and ordained you, that ye should go and
bring forth fruit, and that your fruit should remain: that whatsoever ye shall ask of the
Father in my name, he may give it to you. These things I command you, that ye love
one another* (John 15:13-17).

I'm striving to be a friend like Jesus. I'm the friend who will go
out of my way to do or be there for anyone. I display acts of kindness
and support to complete strangers, co-workers, and neighbors in the
same manner as I do toward those I love and trust. I don't do this for
recognition but for the love of God that's within my heart. I just love

God's people. When I see someone in need, I feel it's my duty as a child of God, if I'm able, to supply that need. I believe that when people bring matters of life to us, that is God's way of showing us how to be a solution to the problem.

Often times people who have a giving spirit as I do can be left on the sidelines feeling rejected, used, and betrayed. What we all must remember is that no two people will show appreciation in the same manner. It doesn't mean that we're not appreciated or even unloved; it's simply that people show emotions in different ways. And, the feelings of rejection, mistreatment, or betrayal are thoughts that linger in your conscious. You can choose to not feel those emotions.

I am disturbed by how people have treated each other in this society. I know the things that I'm exposing here in this chapter others feel or have felt. Others have gone and/or are going through the same thing in their friendships. Stay focused on God and he will see you through. I received a revelation one night while in prayer, God said: people aren't rejecting you, they're rejecting the God who lives in you. That gave me a whole new perspective, and I will always remember those words. Then the Lord revealed the scripture to me found in Luke 10:16 which states: *He who hears you hears me, he who rejects you rejects me, and he who rejects me rejects Him who sent me.* Now, that was a phenomenal revelation.

I've learned through the grace of God what it means to be a friend, and also the type of friend I want to have in my life. I learned that I can be loving, compassionate, understanding, giving, and kind-hearted. I can have friendships with God-fearing individuals who share common goals and dreams; that's God's will for my life.

There have been times in my friendships that I haven't been the way I previously described because I became frustrated by the way people treated me. I've been selfish, uncaring, insensitive, and just plain mean. I got tired of being the nice gal all the time and getting nothing in return. That was my first mistake: I was a friend who was only nice so that I could receive the same in return. What I've since learned is that I must be kind just because that's what I am called to be, not for what I may receive in return.

Today, I derive great pleasure from giving to others, especially when I can do it in secret. I like the feeling I get from giving to others what God has richly blessed me with. I know all that I have has come from God and I'm thankful because I also recognize that he didn't have to give me anything at all. Praise the Lord.

I've been blessed to have a lot of good people come into my life over the years. I've maintained friendships with several people for more than ten years.

I want to share with you from the book of 2 Peter 1:5-8, where it states: *And beside this, giving all diligence, add to your faith virtue; and to virtue knowledge; And to knowledge temperance; and to temperance patience; and to patience godliness; And to godliness brotherly kindness; and to brotherly kindness charity. For if these things be in you, and abound, they make you that ye shall neither be barren nor unfruitful in the knowledge of our Lord Jesus Christ.*

That scripture spoke to the friend in me and I pray that it's speaking to the friend in you right now. To practice diligence, virtue, knowledge, temperance, patience, godliness, kindness, and charity is to truly be a friend to someone.

As I stated earlier, I've been blessed with many long-term friendships. I have several people in my life that I classify as friends because we've been there for one another many times over the years, enduring both the good and the bad.

My closest friends are Dawn, Romona, Doretha, Jasmine, Lasonja, Lauren, and Lamont. They listen when I need someone to talk to. They make me laugh. They make me smile! I know they're my friends because they love me for who I am today! For these reasons and many more, I consider each one of my friends a **gift** from God!

I pray that whoever is reading this book has experienced the joy of a divine friendship and if you have not, may you someday experience the joy that comes along with someone who is a *true* friend.

Today, in my friendships, I don't go along for the ride. I'm an active participant in the relationship. Friendships are relationships in another sense of the word. It's a relationship that for some people will outlast marriage, divorce, death, and many other challenges of life. A friend is still there when the sun doesn't shine, willing to hold your hand or give a hug just when you need it most. A friend loves you just as you are, even when you're not at your best. Whether you're fat or skinny, rich or poor, in good spirits or bad, she is still your friend and loves you the same. A friend is also one who strengthens you with prayers, blesses you with love, and encourages you with hope.

For those who may not have a friend on earth, I want to tell you that you always have a friend in Jesus. He loves you no matter what. He wants to recognize that he is wherever you are. He will dry your tears when you cry, comfort you when you're sad, hold you when you're lonely, stand beside you in the midst of a trial or tribulation, and best of all he'll never leave you or forsake you (Hebrews 13:5). Now that's what I call a *best friend.*

If you've never experienced a "best friends" relationship with the Lord, here are some steps that may help you reunite with Him or establish the friendship you've always longed for:

1. Assign Him first place every day, making Him your first priority in all things.
2. Adore and cherish Him as the One you want to *be with* and *be like.* Allow Him into your life by sharing the little things. The Bible says, *"pour out your heart"* to Him (Psalm 62:8).
3. Aspire to grow in your friendship with Him. Set goals for your relationship with God. Where do you want to be with Him two months from now . . . and two years from now?

I've found that if I make it a priority to be with God every day, share my secrets and experiences with Him and keep the friendship alive, He is to me someone who sticks closer than a brother, closer than a best friend (Proverbs 18:24). It becomes a desire deep down on the inside to please God; not a chore but something you will long to do because of all He has done for you.

My prayer is that if you haven't acknowledged Jesus in your life already, that by the time you've finished reading this book, you'll be inspired to broaden your consciousness and turn within to recognize and obey the indwelling presence of God.

Life After the Pain

Chapter 16

Surrender to God's Will & Forgive

Romans 12:2
And be not conformed to this world:
but be ye transformed by the renewing of your mind,
that ye may prove what is that good,
and acceptable, and perfect, will of God.

Forgiveness is a subject many will not want to face or discuss, especially survivors of abuse. The last thing former victims want to hear is, "It's time to forgive those who have hurt you in the past." At least that's how I felt for years and I think if you're honest with yourself, you have felt the same way.

The first step to making this task a reality is to surrender your *all* to God. I don't know any way around it because without Him, it's virtually impossible to walk in the spirit of forgiveness.

In December 1997, after fourteen years, I finally surrendered my will over to the will of God for my life. I humbled myself before God, and he not only forgave me but also imparted a spirit of forgiveness upon my heart for others.

The following scripture found in 1 Peter 4:8 states: *And above all things have fervent charity among yourselves: for charity shall cover the multitude of sins.* This scripture speaks to the forgiveness in our hearts for those who may have hurt us in the past. The bible speaks a multitude of times concerning forgiveness.

The first person I needed to forgive was myself. I needed to realize that the abuse I sustained in my life wasn't my fault. I didn't ask to be abused nor did I deserve it in any way. I also needed to forgive myself for the shame of prostitution that has plagued me for over fifteen years.

The next person I needed to forgive was my mother, for not being a parent when I needed her the most. I forgive her neglect and the denial she continues to live with. Without Christ, without an understanding of her need for divine help, she is a victim of her own hatred, bitterness, and guilt. For all I know, my mother is going through her own private hell, a torment for which she knows no escape. Keeping that in mind makes it easier to forgive her.

The last person I desperately needed to forgive was my stepfather for the thirteen years of abuse and its effect upon my life thereafter. I realize that anyone who could harm an innocent child does not recognize the Christ within.

I still want my family to be a part of my life, but they do not choose to be an active part of my life. My stepfather and mother are still together. People often wonder and ask why I still want them to be a part of my life and I say the bottom line, for me, is, *they are still my family!*

My fellow sisters/brothers in Christ, I want to follow after David's example in the bible. In the New Testament Acts 13:22 it states: *And when he had removed him, he raised up unto them David to be their king; to whom also he gave testimony, and said, I have found David the son of Jesse, a man after mine own heart, which shall fulfill all my will.* Take notice to the last portion of that scripture where it states that David was a man after God's own heart.

I'd like to consider myself a woman after God's own heart. My heart is in the right place for I desire to do the will of God in all aspects of my life and I use every opportunity possible to spread joy to others.

In 1 Samuel 16:7 the bible states,...*for the Lord seeth not as man seeth; for man looketh on the outward appearance, but the Lord looketh on the heart.*

It's time to get our hearts in order, not tomorrow but right now. For the Lord states in the book of Jeremiah 17:10: *I the Lord search the heart, I try the reins, even to give every man according to his way, and according to the fruit of his doings.*

I welcome the Lord to search my heart and to chastise me when I'm not living under his will. For the bible also speaks to us about the things that we allow to flow out of our mouths. Some things that we say do not uplift but can, in fact, tear someone down.

Jesus is in the business of lifting and restoring people, and we should all be in that same business today! Cutting someone down to lift you up is the lowest form of ego gratification. Don't do it! It's a huge sign of insecurity.

Before you examine anybody else, examine yourself! Do you have the same challenge, or another one that's just as bad? Have you succeeded where you're accusing another of failing? In other words, have you earned the right to speak? Listen to these words spoken in Ephesians 4:15: *But speaking the truth in love, may (we) grow up into him in all things, which is the head, even Christ.*

To those people who believe that I act like I'm better than anyone else is, I say this: I am a child of God, nothing more and nothing less! I want to share with you a scripture that clearly indicates no man is better than another is, and we're all alike in the eyes of God. The scripture is Romans 3:23 and it states: *For all have sinned, and come short of the glory of God.* The scripture doesn't say that some have sinned, it clearly states that *all* have sinned and fallen short of his glory.

I also know that the word of God instructs that once you begin to work for the Lord, persecution will come for his name's sake. Ever since October 18, 1998, when I was baptized with the Holy Ghost and blessed with the power of God, quite a few people do not associate with me.

This scripture concerning persecution is especially important to me, found in John 15:20: *Remember the word that I said unto you, The servant is not greater than his lord. If they have persecuted me, they will also persecute you; if they have kept my saying, they will keep yours also. But all these things will they do unto you for my name's sake, because they know not him that sent me.*

Another reason certain people have chosen not to associate with me is because I'm not going to condone their behavior. I call it as I see it and attempt to minister to their spirit in hopes of encouraging them to live their lives according to the will of God. However, when they aren't receptive and choose not to talk with me, I let go and let God take over.

Initially my feelings were hurt, but I found peace in Jesus. I was set free from that burden and those relationships have been replaced with healthier relationships.

God does take care of the desires of our hearts when we live under his will. For the book of Psalm 37:4-5 states: *Delight thyself also in the Lord; and he shall give thee the desires of thine heart. Commit thy way unto the Lord; trust also in him; and he shall bring it to pass.*

As you have seen, I continually refer to scriptures when I speak of the Lord because I am continually striving to live by his word. I want you to know exactly how important it is for us to seek out his word for our lives. It's about loving people, once you've come to this awareness to expand their awareness of Christ and recognize the power of God within that we all possess.

I want you to remember that you should never let anyone talk down to you for allowing God's will in your life.

God's word instructs us: *Love your enemies, bless them that curse you, do good to them that hate you, and pray for them which despitefully use you, and persecute you* (Matthew 5:44). The reason I keep going back to this point is because it's critical.

It's very easy to love those who love us and to forgive those who forgive us – but it takes faith to love and forgive those who do not love and forgive us. *For even the tax collectors do that much* (love those who love you) (Matthew 5:46).

Forgiveness frees me from the past and moves me forward in life. Jesus understood clearly and taught others the healing power of forgiveness. How good it feels to be free of burdens that have weighed upon us and caused us emotional harm. And how relieved I feel because I realize that I can forgive and be forgiven.

Because I forgive myself and others of perceived hurts and slights, I am no longer tied to the past. I move forward in life to the present time and enjoy divine health, happiness, and prosperity. I enhance the relationships that have been established already and also the relationships that are just becoming established.

My heart has personally been convicted by this scripture found in Matthew 6:14-15: *For if ye forgive men their trespasses, your heavenly Father will also forgive you: But if ye forgive not men their trespasses, neither will your Father forgive your trespasses.*

No matter what happened yesterday or last week or last year, today is a fresh start for me. I declare and believe that today is a new beginning for me. Thank you, God.

I put aside regrets about what I did or did not do in the past and live for joy and the wonder of today. There will never again be a time when I can experience what this moment holds, so I open my mind and heart to the wondrous blessings that are awaiting my discovery.

God created me to live a life of wonder, so right now is the perfect time for me to live as God intends me to live. Today truly is the first day of a new beginning for me.

Life After the Pain

Need I say more? God richly bless!

Epilogue

2 Corinthians 5:17
Therefore if any man be in Christ,
he is a new creature:
old things are passed away;
behold, all things are become new.

Lord, help me focus on one important fact: The battle does not belong to me, but to God. I will praise thee, O Lord, with my whole heart; I will show forth all thy marvellous works. I will be glad and rejoice in thee: I will sing praise to thy name, O thou most High (Psalm 9:1-2).

The Lord also will be a refuge for the oppressed, a refuge in times of trouble. And they that know thy name will put their trust in thee: for thou, Lord, hast not forsaken them that seek thee (Psalm 9:9-10).

The mission behind this work is to break the silence of abuse in my life and show the world that God is merciful and full of grace to heal and deliver us from the bondage of our past.

Repeatedly, God has shown me that my experiences are to help others work through the hurts of their pasts. One aching heart knows when another is aching and my experiences enable me to understand how others feel. These aren't empty words; they're filled with love and compassion for you as fellow survivors. Of course, not everyone who reads this book is a survivor and to you I want to say, "thank you for your support."

In light of that, I'd like to share this scripture found in 2 Corinthians 1:4: *Who comforteth us in all our tribulation, that we may be able to comfort them which are in any trouble, by the comfort wherewith we ourselves are comforted of God.* That scripture is a clear indication that we endure certain things in life so that God may use us to comfort one another should an opportunity present itself.

My conviction was the starting point for me in putting a shattered life back together and learning to develop a personal relationship with the indwelling presence of God within. With Christ, those who are caught in bitterness and rejection can make it. The scripture found in Luke 4:18-19 states: *The spirit of the Lord is upon me, because he hath anointed me to preach the gospel to the poor; he hath sent me to heal the brokenhearted, to preach deliverance to the captives, and recovering of sight to the blind, to set at liberty them that are bruised, to preach the acceptable year of the Lord.* The key point to capture from this scripture is that Christ has ointment for the bruises and wounds of the soul. He wants to heal your pain if only you will *believe* that he is able.

The Bible says in 2 Corinthians 12:10, *Therefore I take pleasure in infirmities, in reproaches, in necessities, in persecutions, in distresses for Christ's sake: for when I am weak, then am I strong.* This scripture is a clear indication that everything we may go through in life can be used for the glorification of God. If you are just coming to terms with your past, you may not agree with this. However, I assure you that if you *surrender* it all over to the care of God, he will see you through.

Whatever questions you dare to ask, whatever methods and changes you decide upon, keep in mind that my answers will not necessarily be yours. I faithfully bring you back to the word of God because that's what has worked for me. I know that every situation I go through, someone already went through it long ago. A scripture can be found for every moment and every feeling that you could ever have.

Setting ourselves free is an individual process done exclusively by God. As we make our decisions, experiencing both challenges and victories, we can offer compassion not only to ourselves, but also to others. We can embrace and live with men/women who decide differently than us, not needing to criticize and change them, and not playing the voice of God in their lives.

"You, my [brother/sister], are called to be free." The entire law is summed up in a single command: *Love your neighbor as yourself* (Matthew 19:19, Galatians 5:14). So the Lord says to Walk in the Spirit, and you shall not fulfill the lust of the flesh (Galatians 5:16). Following this biblical advice, we can refuse to judge and openly love our spiritual sisters and brothers just as they are.

The life of absolute surrender is unfeigned obedience to God, fellowship with His word, and prayer. Such life has two sides: absolute surrender to do what God wants us to do, and letting God work what He wants to do.

To do what God wants us to do, we *must give up ourselves* to the will of God. We must say to the Lord God: "By your grace I desire to do your will in everything, every moment of every day." God wants to bless us in a way beyond what we expect. As the scripture reads in Jeremiah 33:3: *Call unto me, and I will answer thee, and show thee great and mighty things, which thou knowest not.*

For sixteen years I struggled against the idea of absolute surrender, thinking it frightening and unfair, as if God couldn't be trusted with my life. I've grown to understand that surrender isn't a punishment, but the gateway to joy. It sets us on a path filled with God's spiritual blessings. It's God who enables us to carry out the surrender.

I discovered, too, that when the Master brings us to surrender, our hearts are melted and our eyes are opened so with relief we say, "Yes, Lord, I understand it now. I'll give this up. It's hurting me and you want to heal and free me." I finally comprehended that I'm surrendering to a lover of my soul, not to a dictator. Unfortunately, before we understand this, many of us run away, believing there's nothing better than what we clutch in our hands. Often what we cling to can gradually destroy us.

In Romans 5:3-5 the scripture states: *And not only so, but we glory in tribulations also: knowing that tribulation worketh patience; And patience, experience; and experience, hope; And hope maketh not ashamed; because the love of God is shed abroad in our hearts by the Holy Ghost which is given unto us.* This is an awesome word from God! For his word is making it clear that no matter what we may go through, something good can always be obtained from it. We can never have enough patience and hope for we know that's all a part of the mere experience.

Believe me, I still have plenty of character dysfunctions that need God's touch, but He promises if I keep surrendering to Him, they'll be replaced with the fruit of His spirit. This fruit is the quality of inner beauty: love, joy, peace, longsuffering, gentleness, goodness, faith, meekness, and temperance (Galatians 5:22). Paul reminded believers that, *"And they that are Christ's have crucified the flesh with the affections and lusts. If we live in the Spirit, let us walk in the Spirit."* (Galatians 5:24-25). When we apply this scripture in our lives, we are then able to cultivate the fruit of the Spirit into our lifestyles.

Yet it's still our decision as to whether God can cultivate His glorious beauty in us. Even if we've discovered our family's influences on

92

us; if we've learned that God didn't desire for us to be abused; if we've considered how to be less obsessive about our past, we still need to choose whether we'll surrender to God and His transforming power or continue wallowing in our memories of the past.

It's my hope that in the way we look, the reason we act, and what we choose, we will serve the Lord.

God gave humanity free will; not even He can transform us unless we give Him permission. If we really desire to change, if we want release from our bondage, then with the supernatural power of the Holy Spirit, we can change from the inside out. We can choose to let go of the painful memories from the past. We can walk in freedom, becoming spiritually healthy, happy, and prosperous.

Yet the responsibility to change rests on our shoulders; no one can do the work for us. If you want to change your attitudes about the past, whether they are small alterations or big transformations, it's up to you. Whatever the case it's important to begin doing something and it's crucial that God rather than man guide these activities. You can pray to Him, *"The Lord is my light and my salvation; whom shall I fear? The Lord is the strength of my life; of whom shall I be afraid?"* (Psalm 27:1). And He will answer, *"And thine ears shall hear a word behind thee, saying, This is the way, walk ye in it."*

Serving God is a daily job. Twenty-four hours a day, *seven* days a week and it's never a dull moment. Someone told me once that, "Serving God is boring." I'm feeling more excitement and peace serving God than I ever felt serving the world! I never have a dull moment in my life for if I'm not in church, ministering to someone in need, reading a good book, watching a good movie, or listening to music, I'm reading the word.

One night in a dream, I saw a centrally located center that was set up for women, men, and children who have been abused in one form or another, and for teenage runaways. I'm praying that dream will come to pass and be a welcome center for those individuals who have the need for spiritual support. I eagerly aspire to be used by God to bring this national crisis to a halt. I want to provide knowledge to the world on how it feels to be abused but also that the world may see, "We can overcome." We don't have to be victims our entire lives. We do not have to allow our past to continue dictating our future. Jesus is ready and willing to set us free. And, my mission here on earth is to break the silence of abuse…one life at a time.

Believe it or not, I also see myself ministering to rape and child abuse offenders who are incarcerated. I feel the need to reach out to them with the love and word of God. I want them to know they can right their wrongs by surrendering their lives to Jesus Christ. They are entitled to rehabilitation, if that's what they desire to receive.

When serving God and allowing Him to be the divine Sovereign of your life, you never know what you may end up doing. I consider myself a chosen vessel; God is the Owner and I am the Manager. And, together we make a wonderful team, because one plus God equals a majority.

I serve a mighty God who's able to do all things if only I believe, and I do. There is nothing too hard for God (Jeremiah 32:27). I know too much about him to doubt him at this point. I've seen his marvelous wonders.

I pray that what I've shared in this book has touched your heart in a special way. God is good all the time and all the time God is good. I pray that if you couldn't use all of it, maybe you could just use a part of it. I urge you that if this book has blessed you, go out and pick up a copy for a friend to support this important mission.

For me, it's about doing God's work! It's about teaching people to recognize the power of God within that is ready and willing to heal the wounds of the past. This book is intended to plant a seed in the hearts of many and even aid in other ministries to broaden people's awareness. It's intended solely to glorify Almighty God. In the end, it is God alone who gives the increase (1 Corinthians 3:6).

We need more testimonials published so this society will stop ignoring the issues of abuse and start doing something to protect our people. It has been ignored far too long. Too many innocent children have fallen to the hands of rapists and abusers. Too many women and men have fallen prey to stalkers, including their own husbands and wives.

People have cried out for help and nobody has listened. The statistical percentages haven't dropped, but increased. We must send a message to the world that we're not going to sit by and watch anymore; we're going to stand up and demand that our voices be heard.

How long will we allow this to continue? How many more children must die at the hands of an abusive parent? How many more little girls/boys will be raped by their parents, while we sit on the sidelines? How many more women/men will be brutally slain by their spouses? How many serial killers will remain at large? How much more can we take of this? When will we, as Christians, step up to the plate and make a difference in someone's life?

Abuse has become an epidemic in our society. People are frustrated and children are suffering because of it. Children need our love and help today, for they are our future. If we don't help them, who will?

Will we continue to wait for someone else to step up and help or will we take the initiative today to make a difference in a child's life? It may be a child you know in need. If not there are places all over the world that need help taking care of children from broken homes. Broken homes of abuse, divorce, and death. Children crying out for someone to show that they care.

The past is the past for me; it's too late to go back and change what has happened. It's not too late, however, for another child. Thus, in essence, if I leave anything with you, I encourage you to reach out to someone else in need.

I realize that sometimes it's easier to say than to do, but through the grace of God restoring us from our past, we are able to move on with our lives. I heard a pastor say one day that we as Christians need to stop looking for a blessing and start *being* a blessing to someone!

It's important that we not make our past our only focus in life; instead, we must fill our minds with positive thoughts of what the future holds for survivors. If you can only believe in God, I assure you that everything else will be just fine.

No one can count the blessings God has for you! You must hold onto the hand of God now more than ever because your reading this book was not by accident or coincidence; a change is about to take place in your life. God is not blind to any abusive situation and he can turn it around for your good.

Do not be blinded in your spirit by things happening in the natural. God said, "I will go before thee, and make the crooked places straight" (Isaiah 45:2). The biggest struggle you are facing can be won. What seems tough to you is weak and small to God.

The light of God's truth can eradicate something out of your past, which has seemed to follow you! Do not carry yesterday's baggage into tomorrow! Do not poison your future with the pain of the past. You need the word of God filling your mind like a fresh summer breeze...now! God's word purifies! It delivers! It renews! It energizes! It sets the captives free! It brings peace and joy! It shines light in darkness!

Remember, think big because you serve a big God! No thought should be small! My biggest dream is to take a complete tour of Israel. I desire to walk where my Savior has walked! I want to be baptized where he was baptized! I'm thinking big and believing God will make provisions for me to go and it won't be long! Amen.

Finally, my sisters/brothers, I've been instructed by God to share with you the steps you can take to begin recognizing and obeying the indwelling presence of God. Deliverance is possible, but it isn't cheap. Jesus Christ paid with his life, so that salvation could be offered to us free of charge. God has provided salvation on a basis that permits an individual who can make a decision to have it. God made his salvation available on the basis of a *personal faith* that even a child can exercise. In this respect, everyone is then reduced to the same level in the eyes of God, for all must come to Him on the same terms. The point as brought out in his word is that *God is no respecter of persons* (Acts 10:34).

Many people will not believe the simplicity of salvation. People often feel that they must do something to earn or deserve such a wonderful offer. Yes, something was done so that salvation could be offered to us freely, but Jesus did it all. All that God asks of us is that we believe that Jesus died for our sins and that we receive Him into our heart and life by faith. The genuineness and the reality of your faith will be demonstrated by the transformation of your life.

For by your faith you can claim salvation. The scripture found in Ephesians 2:8-9 states: *For by grace are ye saved through faith; and that not of yourselves: it is the gift of God. Not of works, lest any man should boast.*

Have you discovered that doing things your own way is not working…that, in reality, life is out of control? Perhaps you're even asking, "Why am I here?" At this moment you have the choice of yielding control of your life to the One who created you, loves you, and knows all about you – past, present, and future. If you open your heart to Him, you will see that God has a personalized plan which includes not only His purpose for creating you, but also His promise to fulfill you…to satisfy the deepest hungers of your heart.

To know God's plan, you must recognize your responsibilities as Children of God:

1. Right Thinking
2. Right Feelings
3. Right Words
4. Right Actions
5. Right Reactions

Jesus said: "*I stand at the door and knock,* (your heart's door). *If any man hear my voice and open the door, I will come in to him*" (Revelation 3:20).

Wherever you are
right now, be still.
Right now, you may
pray this simple prayer
asking with all
your heart for
transformation to
take place in your life.
Turn off any music
you may be listening to,
turn the ringers off
on the telephone
(if you can),
and be *very* quiet.

This is going to help
you get in tune with
the Spirit of God.

Feel free to pray this
Prayer Meditation
over and over again,
at any time you need
a lift-me-up in
your spirit.

Prayer Meditation:
Father Mother God, we turn within recognizing the only power in the Universe, God the good, omnipotent. Relax every muscle in your body and tune into the presence of God within right now. Feel its blood running through your veins. Feel its air filling your lungs. Feel the vibration of its heart beating through yours. Be still.

Feel the presence of God fill your entire being with the peace that surpasses all understanding. Feel its presence engulf you with all the blessings God wants you to have. Be still.

Right now, begin to visualize your blessings already in place. Feel your healing taking place right now as you are in tune with the presence of God within. See your finances beginning to increase as you allow yourself the freedom of this meditation.

Recognize right now that there is but one presence and one Power in the universe, God the good, omnipotent, the everywhere – present spirit of absolute good.

In God there is no lack or limitation, I want you to allow all your cares to be cast upon God because He does care for you very much. God has awesome plans for your life and you have nothing to fear. God is your Shepherd, you shall not want for nothing.

As you turn within honoring the presence of God that you are experiencing at this very moment, give thanks to God for all he has done and will do in your life and for your new level of awareness you have felt this day.

And so it is. Amen.

Now believe (John 3:36) Jesus to keep his promise and show your trust in Him, by simply thanking Him for what He promised He would do. Thank you so much for so much, God.

This is God's way of salvation according to His word. You have asked (Matthew 7:7), and believed (John 3:36). Take God at His word today. For as the scripture found in 1 Peter 1:25 states: *But the word of the Lord endureth forever. And this is the word which by the gospel is preached unto you.*

Child of God, whatever you do, don't give up! With God's help you can rebuild what has been previously torn down by abuse. Whatever happened yesterday is in the past. God's grace and mercy are new every morning (Lamentations 3:23). Today He's saying to you, "You can start over again, and this time I will enable you to win!" Only then, will you begin to see *life after the pain* for yourself. Remember, whatever bridge you may need to cross, Jesus is the bridge to life! He is the answer to our challenges as we face them, day to day.

Life After the Pain

I want to hear from you about what reading this book has done for your life. I want to know, did you pray the prayer of salvation? And how has God begun to transform your life? Please contact me and share your testimony of what the Lord has done in your life.

You may send your testimonials and/or order additional copies of this book to:

Life After the Pain
c/o Blanca Romero
P.O. Box 171
Belcamp, Maryland 21017

If placing an order for additional copies of the book, please enclose $12.00 per copy, in addition to $2.00 for shipping and handling. Please include with your order: your name, address, city, state, and zip code. Make your check or money order payable to Blanca Romero. Please remember to allow two weeks for delivery of your order.

May God's grace, mercy, love, and peace be with you always. Thank you for your support. Remember, I'll be praying for you. I love you and may God richly bless you!!!